ROUTLEDGE LIBRARY EDITIONS:
WOMEN AND BUSINESS

Volume 10

WOMEN AT WORK

WOMEN AT WORK

A Brief Introduction to Trade Unionism for Women

MARY AGNES HAMILTON

Routledge
Taylor & Francis Group

LONDON AND NEW YORK

First published in 1941 by George Routledge & Sons, Ltd.

This edition first published in 2017
by Routledge
2 Park Square, Milton Park, Abingdon, Oxon OX14 4RN

and by Routledge
711 Third Avenue, New York, NY 10017

Routledge is an imprint of the Taylor & Francis Group, an informa business

British Library Cataloguing in Publication Data
A catalogue record for this book is available from the British Library

ISBN: 978-1-138-23710-0 (Set)
ISBN: 978-1-315-27106-4 (Set) (ebk)
ISBN: 978-1-138-24316-3 (Volume 10) (hbk)
ISBN: 978-1-138-28088-5 (Volume 10) (pbk)
ISBN: 978-1-315-27182-8 (Volume 10) (ebk)

Publisher's Note
The publisher has gone to great lengths to ensure the quality of this reprint but points out that some imperfections in the original copies may be apparent.

Disclaimer
The publisher has made every effort to trace copyright holders and would welcome correspondence from those they have been unable to trace.

WOMEN AT WORK

A Brief Introduction to
Trade Unionism for
Women

By

MARY AGNES HAMILTON

LONDON

GEORGE ROUTLEDGE & SONS, LTD.

BROADWAY HOUSE : 68–74 CARTER LANE, E.C.4

First published 1941

Printed in Great Britain by Butler & Tanner Ltd., Frome and London

CONTENTS

FOREWORD

This small book does not attempt to give a picture of the work of women in war. For that, the time is not yet. It is concerned to relate the argument for Trade Unionism to the needs of women who work, whether in their homes or outside them ; its facts and figures refer to pre-war conditions.

It is, in part, history, and a history of selfless, corporate endeavour of which women may well be proud as may the men who have been and are to-day their partners in it. In so far as it is history, however, its subject is a great and growing force whose future cannot be measured in terms of its present. War conditions are again, as in 1914–18, changing the range and scope of the employment of women ; if the position of the woman war worker is to-day fairer and more favourable than it was a quarter of a century ago, she has Trade Union action to thank for it.

To anyone to whom such a topic seems, at this time, inappropriate, this may be said : The pattern of the society we hope to see emerge after this war will differ, in many respects, from the pattern that exists to-day. But, if it is to bring the good life in wider measure and over a more generous range than the old, it will do so by holding fast to certain values. It happens that any study of women, and of Trade Unions, must force some of these essential values to the front. Central and essential among them is respect for the human being as such, regardless of colour, creed, race or sex. On this, every claim by women for equal treatment rests.

Foreword

Lincoln said a State cannot exist half slave and half free. No more can a Trade Union. By the logic of its own being, it is compelled to think not in terms of men workers and of women workers, but of workers. Nor is this all. The association of workers for collective negotiation presumes reliance on the civilised method of argument and co-operation, not the barbaric method of force ; it also presumes the practice of making binding engagements on the strength of the given word. It is a mark of the free man that he can rely on such contract, and of the free State that it upholds it.

So, women in the State, like Trade Unions in the State, symbolise and represent the recognition by the community of standards at once positive and creative. To examine the place of either in our common life is to be recalled sharply to the human values from which the struggle to master its resources and mechanics derives its worth: human values now threatened as never before with black obliteration. Nothing of accident in the fact that Totalitarianism first suppresses Trade Unions and then goes on to degrade women to breeders of cannon fodder who have no need to think. Perhaps the one service the challenge we are now meeting has done us lies here—we know, now, in what we believe.

Of the inadequacy and incompleteness of this small contribution to so great a theme, the writer is keenly aware. No body of people are more generous with time and help than the busy secretaries and organisers of the Unions. If the field of women's employment is here imperfectly covered, the fault does not lie with them, but with conditions of work that prevented me from going to see them. To those who did assist me, in the early stages, my warm thanks go out ; to those whom I was prevented from consulting, my apologies,

Foreword

I have, as is obvious, drawn freely both on Barbara Drake's classic study of *Women in Trade Unions,* and on G. D. H. Cole's most useful *British Trade Unionism Today* ; as, of course, on the annual Reports of the Trades Union Congress. I owe a special debt of gratitude to Herbert Tracey, for most generously given help. If errors of fact and heresies of interpretation appear, they are wholly my own.

CHELSEA,
   February 1941.

B

CHAPTER I

BACKGROUND OF FACT

WORK is the common lot of women, as of men. The ninety per cent. of the population which is roughly described as belonging to the working class is correctly so described. It includes most women, as most men.

The picture of the world we live in, however, is generally drawn by, and for, and from, the small proportion of society in which the earnings or inheritance of the man permit him to keep his women-folk at leisure, or engaged in occupations chosen for some non-economic reason. Hence there has come to exist a view that the working woman is the exception. She is, admittedly, very important in time of war. Then, a lot is heard of her. Then, she is necessary, and seen to be necessary, to the nation's effort. Actually, of course, she is as necessary in peace-time : so is the work she does. But a community which measures in terms of money recognises, normally, as work only the work paid for in cash.

Since the pages that follow will be concerned mainly with that section of working women who do earn money for their work, it is necessary to stress at the outset the fact that the paid workers are but a small section of the army of women who work for their living. What is peculiar in the position of the woman worker is that, while she is still young—generally under 25— she changes over from one kind of work to another. She expects this to happen. Society expects it to happen. It does not, as a matter of fact, by any means always happen. There were, in 1931, a million and a half more women than men. A large proportion of women, therefore, do not marry. Nevertheless, the expectation of marriage colours the outlook and the experience of the normal woman. Marriage, where it occurs, does not in most cases mean that she stops working. On the contrary, most women go on working, as men go on working, all their lives long. Only the kind and circumstances of their work change.

This transfer from paid to unpaid work is the great governing circumstance in the life and condition of women. It is called " ceasing to be employed on marriage ". But, for the vast majority, that phrase is an entirely false description of what, in fact, occurs. False in fact, the description is also false in implication. To the nation, the work done by women after marriage in their homes is quite as important as any work done in factory, field or office. Factory, field and office work are there in order to sustain and make possible a decent life in the home. The home is the focus of value. It is what the rest is for. This is true and, in words, admitted to be true, where there are children. No one who thinks for a single moment denies that what they are given in the home is an indispensable and vital element in the sound growth of the nation. Its hopes are located in their minds and bodies, and the background in which those minds and bodies grow depends on the woman who makes it. What is not so fully recognised is that even where there are no children the home-maker is contributing an element to the life of the nation not only in the domestic work she does, but in the atmosphere which only she can create. The power to do the work of the home, in this wider sense, including as it does elements of very various character and skill, is not, of course, the " natural " endowment of every woman, just because she is a woman. Here is a craft, like another, taking patience, self-discipline and hard work for its accomplishment, and demanding certain aptitudes. Women, no less than men, have often failed to rate it as high as, socially, it deserves to be rated. They fail largely because to this craft no scale of payment is related ; and we all think, consciously or unconsciously, in terms of payment.

Actually, in every attempted description of the work of women—and this will be no exception—the largest area of normal female employment is, perforce, omitted. In a small proportion of homes in Britain, women are employed for payment to do the work of cooking, washing, cleaning without which the great national machine of necessary work could not function. More than a million and a half women do paid domestic service. Something over ten million women are doing unpaid domestic service. They sew, they wash, they scrub, they cook, they mend and make clothes for themselves and the children and the breadwinner. In the country, they look after garden and animals. Without break or holiday, their work goes on. It is " never done ". If it stopped, the entire machine would run down. Although they do not themselves earn wages, their interest in wage-rates and working conditions is as direct and acute as that of the wage-earner ; their entire life depends on and is governed by the standards that are secured by those who do earn wages.

In 1911, the Census taken every ten years, which gives the best available picture of the life of the nation at work, made the startling innovation of counting as

" occupied " the women working in their homes at work for which they would have been paid if they had been doing it in other people's homes. Normally, however, as in 1931 (the last available counting), " occupied ", for the Census, means not working but working for cash : what the Americans call " Gainfully employed ". Unless this is borne in mind, an entirely unreal picture of the working world emerges. With this precaution well in mind, it is possible to look at the 1931 Census figures, since they give the broad background of fact.

In 1931, the population of Great Britain comprised 16,410,894 women and 14,632,859 men over the age of 14. Since it was by then illegal to employ anyone under the age of 14, these figures cover the country's employable force. In this force of 31 millions in round figures, women outnumbered men by more than $1\frac{1}{2}$ millions—a fact of no small significance when what is called the " incidence of marriage " on the employment of women comes to be considered.

The Census showed that out of $14\frac{1}{2}$ million men, $13\frac{1}{4}$ millions were " occupied " ; out of $16\frac{1}{2}$ million women, $5\frac{1}{2}$ millions were " occupied ".

When the total figure of occupied women is broken up into its main groups, it is seen that the large blocks are as follows :

Personal Service : 1,936,978. This covers domestic service, laundry work and charing, the largest group being Domestic Service with 1,332,224.
Factory Employment : 1,855,586.
Commercial Employment : 604,833.
Clerical Employment : 579,359.
Professional Employment : 389,359.

Although these groupings, taken from the Census, do not correspond closely with the lines of Trade Union organisation, they do show, at a glance, the main distribution of the paid employment of women, and show, too, the great main problem presented to the Trade Union organiser—the fact that less than one-third of the employed women are in Factory employment. In other words, two-thirds of them are mainly isolated, and not group workers. These Census figures, while important, by no means reveal the full facts about the " gainful " employment of women. In the case of women, it is necessary to remember that occupation, in the Census use of that term, is much more irregularly spaced out over the years of life than is the case with men. A man normally enters the occupation by which he earns his living when his education finishes ; in the vast majority of cases, therefore, at 14 plus. In it he normally continues until he is 65 or even 70. A woman, on the other hand, normally enters occupation, as he does, when her education finishes, but she does not stay in it. Thus, the proportion of women engaged in paid work is very much higher in the early age-groups than in the middle and later ones. Four women out of every five in England, Scotland and Wales are wage-earners at some period in their lives. Between the ages of 14 and 24, paid occupation is the rule for women as for men. Three-quarters of all girls over 16, and well over three-quarters of girls between 18 and 21, are at paid work. But, by 25, the proportion begins to fall off sharply. Of women between 25 and 34, not much more than a third are at work. Between 35 and 44, the proportion is less than a quarter.

Of this striking employment curve, the simple explanation is of course marriage, which transfers women from the occupied to the unoccupied columns in the Census tables. It is shown in more detail in the figures below : they further indicate that, as between 1911 and 1931, there is an increase in the occupied percentage for every age-group up to 44, and then a falling-off in the age-groups from 45 upwards.

PERCENTAGE OF OCCUPIED WOMEN TO ALL WOMEN

Age-Group				1911 Census Year	1921	1931
14–15	.	.	.	48	44·8	50·8
16–17	.	.	.	67·3	70·8	75·6
18–20	.	.	.	73·8	76·2	78·9
21–24	.	.	.	61·9	62·8	65·1
25–34	.	.	.	33·8	33·4	36·3
35–44	.	.	.	24·1	22·5	24·1
45–54	.	.	.	23·0	20·9	21
55–64	.	.	.	20·3	19·3	17·8
65–	.	.	.	11·4	10·1	8·3

The outstanding feature of this table is its clear indication of the shape of the curve of women's employment. The peak is in the age-groups below 25. At 25, comes a break and a sharp decline. It shows, too, that a steadily increasing proportion of girls go out to work for wages, as boys do, when they leave school. In 1931, in fact, 4 out of every 5 girls under 20 were at work ; under 24, nearly 3 out of every 4.

The actual picture is not the same, of course, for all parts of the country. In mining and rural areas, for example, fewer girls and young women go out to work for wages than in urban and industrial areas, while in the latter the proportion is higher than the figures in the table show. Further light is thrown by taking the numbers, rather than the percentages, of women at work.

8

NUMBERS OF OCCUPIED WOMEN

Age-Group							
14–15	.	.	.	.	.	.	316,352
16–17	.	.	.	.	.	.	532,175
18–20	.	.	.	⁀	.	.	831,756
21–24	.	.	.	.	.	.	941,157
25–29	.	.	.	.	.	.	737,042
30–34	.	.	.	.	.	.	480,097
35–44	.	.	.	.	.	.	723,574
45–54	.	.	.	.	.	.	554,385
55–59	.	.	.	.	.	.	204,553

Here again there is a marked fall between the 25–29 age-group and that which follows it, 30–34 ; although the numbers working up to 29 are still very high ; the big drop is after that age. Between 35 and 44 the numbers rise again.

So, the broad picture is perfectly definite in either case. The big working groups are composed of girls and quite young women. Between the ages of 18 and 20, four-fifths of the girls in the nation are occupied in wage-earning. Between 21 and 24, the proportion is still very high, well over three-fifths. Then, however, it drops sharply as a percentage, although the number of women remaining at work is still high. Youth is thus the outstanding mark of the woman wage-earner. On this point, all the figures tell the same story. In fact, out of the $5\frac{1}{2}$ million women at work in 1931, over $3\frac{1}{4}$ millions were under the age of 30, and more than half under the age of 25.

The social significance of this fact is obvious. Here, too, is revealed by far the most important element in the difficulty of organising women, of which so much is heard. While they are in industry or in any form of paid work, they are at an age, in the main, at which interest in matters outside their own personal life is not apt to be very keen with either sex. Neither boys nor girls between 16 and 24 normally take their responsibilities, as citizens or as wage-earners, as seriously as they later learn to do. They are concerned with other things—above all, with one another. The young worker is never easy material for the organiser. The woman worker is predominantly young.

She is young. Moreover, she does not expect to stay in paid employment. The expectation of going out, whether or no it is realised, acts as a further disturbing factor. When the young worker expects or hopes to go out of employment while still young, the appeal to take work seriously, and to express that seriousness in the form of joining a Union, obviously encounters the highest degree of unconscious resistance.

Marriage causes a man to take his work more seriously, and adds an argument in favour of the action that will help him to improve his situation as a worker. Marriage, for a woman, represents a total change in work and in all the conditions of her life. For her, as for him, it is a normal experience. Yet for her, as not for him, it is an experience that, whether in fact or in anticipation, militates against her entering a Union. She may, in fact, continue in work ; but she does not expect that work to be the same as it was when she was single. Marriage is so important a feature in the life of the working woman that the figures which indicate how far it does in practice take women out of paid employment must here be set down. The over-all percentage of employed married women was under 10 —actually 9·7—at the time of the 1931 Census ; 8·8 in 1921, and 10·3 in 1911. But these over-all figures need to be broken up to show the percentage at the different age-groups, in order to complete the argument.

PERCENTAGE OF OCCUPIED MARRIED WOMEN TO
ALL MARRIED WOMEN

Age					1911	1921	1931
18–20	.	.	.	.	13·5	15	19·5
21–24	.	.	.	.	12·9	13·2	19·2
25–34	.	.	.	.	10·6	9·9	10·4
35–44	.	.	.	.	10·6	9	10·5
45–54	.	.	.	.	10·5	8·8	8·7
55–59 } 60–64 }	.	.	.	.	8·8	7·9 } 6·9 } 7·5	7·1 } 5·7 } 6·6
65–69 } 70–75 }	.	.	.	.	5·7	5·7	3·9

The highest proportion of married women is to be found in the Textile trades. In every trade, however, in which women are employed, married women figure in large numbers. These married women moreover belong to all age-groups ; in industry, those between 35 and 45 represent a considerable number ; as do those in the younger age-groups. The women over 45 are of course to be found mainly in what the Census calls " other and undefined work " : largely in casual and domestic work, very largely in charing. There were in 1931 over 20,000 married women engaged in charing between the ages of 35 and 45, and 19,000 between 45 and 55.

In all grades of work, the employment of married women is on the increase, and this although they are " barred " in certain lines : notably in the civil and municipal services. The reason for this is not, as a rule, inclination. That does operate with the professional woman, and with all those who have through experience achieved skill in their work. Generally, however, the spur is not choice, but necessity. The compelling force is economic. For every woman who stays on in paid work, after marriage, or returns to work, after a brief interval, for the sake of maintaining a high personal living standard, or because she is keenly interested in the work itself, there are tens who go back to work or stay in it because only so can a home and children be cared for. The Textiles are far from being the only trade which exists on the basis of a " family wage " : in other words, pays wages on which the individual worker cannot support a family. There are, therefore, a very large number of women doing double employment, paid and unpaid : running a home in the hours left over from factory or domestic or casual employment.

Then, the very necessity which drives them out to work makes them weak bargainers for its remuneration. Their weakness betrays them, and they are, in turn, accused of under-cutting, and of being hard to organise.

The briefest survey of the background facts of women's work reveals some of its formidable difficulties ; and something of the hardship that too often accompanies it. As Mary Macarthur summed up the position years ago, it remains to-day : " women are difficult to organise because they are badly paid, and they are badly paid because they are difficult to organise." The very severity of their need for organisation is the greatest obstacle to achieving it. Yet this obstacle presented itself to the men who organised the Trade Unions of the early days, and devised in that great system of mutual aid not only a protection for themselves but a force of infinite value for freedom. The next chapter therefore will be devoted to an attempt to answer the questions, What is a Trade Union ? and, What is it for ?

CHAPTER II

A B C OF TRADE UNIONISM

A CENTURY and a half ago, it was illegal for workers to form any kind of association among themselves. Combinations of workers were forbidden by law, and heavy and even savage penalties were imposed on those who attempted to form them. Employers, law or no law, combined ; workers who sought to do so were criminals. This was the rule at a time when the complete change-over in conditions of work brought about by the introduction of steam-power, and the rapid development of the factory system, were causing the most fearful hardships to men, women and even little children, and the exploitation of their labour was unchecked by any kind of factory code. The laws did not help the workers : on the contrary, they repressed them. Yet they were not permitted to try to help themselves by uniting together. The mere charge of administering an illegal Union oath condemned the labourers of Tolpuddle in Dorset to transportation as convicts in 1834. Theirs was no isolated case. In the middle years of the nineteenth century, attempts at organisation, first on a big national scale, and then through smaller groups, were broken again and again, and leaders heavily punished. Early Trade Union history is as rich in martyrs as in heroes.

At last, after long and devoted efforts, the Acts of 1871-6 were passed, and the right of workers to combine together for mutual aid was defined and safeguarded in law. Nevertheless, the early Trade Unions were looked upon with suspicion by the general public, by its powerful pastors and masters, the economists of the day, and even, to a large extent, by workers themselves. The newspapers were hostile ; Parliament was fearful. There was, it was freely suggested, something dark and subversive about Trade Unionism, and something positively un-British about Trade Unionists. Even in the late decades of the nineteenth century, men hesitated to join a Union, because they knew that membership would make it hard for them to get employment. So the movement grew but slowly. In 1898 there were not much more than a million and a half members in the country and over a million of them were concentrated in the North, where a few trades—miners, shipwrights, boilermakers and iron-workers built comparatively strong organisations, as did the Lancashire cotton workers and the railwaymen.

At this stage, of course, except in the Textile trades, there were few women in the Unions. Yet women had taken part, side by side with men, in the early struggles, as they had shared the horrors of the early days of mechanised industry. For them, as for the men, the Industrial Revolution brought vast changes in the places and conditions of their work. But it was not the introduction of steam-power that set them to work. That had been their lot before. The woman who works has always been there, since the days when " Adam delved and Eve spun " ; and her work has not at any time been confined to the walls of her home. But, after the Revolution, the factory took the place of the small, and often domestic, workshop ; the power-loom of the hand-loom. Things which had been made at home were now made in factories ; women moved after the things into the factories. In the years that have passed since, this process has been carried further and further, and has carried with it a steady increase in the number of women working for wages, both inside factories and elsewhere.

Nevertheless, it took a very long time for men, even working men, and for women themselves, and even working women, to realise that women who worked need the help of Trade Unions as much as, or even more than, their male colleagues. The lace, book-binding, tailoring and boot and shoe Unions, like those in the Textiles, took in women workers and took them in on the same terms as men. Yet, during years in which the Textiles gave leaders to the young Trade Union movement, they could persuade few of their fellows to accept women as members, still less to realise how important it was to organise them. The women who saw the need of Unions had to try to organise women separately, although most of them fully realised the weakness of such organisation. Men who believed passionately in the right of workers to associate for their mutual protection, and fought like lions for the freedom to organise, first in this industry and that, turned a deaf ear and an unseeing eye to the needs of women—and to the danger which unorganised women could represent to their own advancing movement. Women were, then as now, as a rule paid less than men ; therefore, men argued, they must, if admitted, pull the men's rates down. Years of struggle and con-tinual argument in Trades Union Congresses had to be gone through before it was realised that the policy of the blind eye to women was more dangerous to the men's standards than that of taking them inside.

The fear of cheap labour was, of course, the main

explanation of this attitude on the part of the Unions. It is still the explanation of the policy pursued by isolated Unions, although one long-abandoned by the main body of Trade Union opinion and practice. It was abandoned largely because it was seen that cheap female labour was most dangerous when it was outside the Union organisation. In fact, so long as women were kept out of organised trades and employments there was no means, for them or for anybody else, of preventing their underpayment, and consequent under-cutting of established rates. They were driven into unorganised trades. There, they pulled low rates down still further. They did not want to be blacklegs. But, so long as they were isolated, they were helpless ; help-less, above all, to prevent themselves from thus injuring their own conditions and those of men. They worked because they had to ; and they worked at starvation rates because their employers dealt with each one individually, on the basis of her dire need of bread for herself and, often, for her children.

Nevertheless, the old-time Trade Unionist's argu-ment against the admission of women was not based wholly on economic grounds. If it had been, it would have been much sooner overcome by the facts. It was a mixture of economics and sentiment. The senti-mental part of it often blinded people—women as well as men—to the economic facts.

Actually, the policy of the barred door was, at the time, part of the habitual thinking of an epoch. Every-body said " Woman's place is the home ", without stopping to inquire whether that home could, or in fact did, provide her with the means whereby to live. So, working men, like middle-class men, felt that woman was not only a peril to their standards in industry and the professions ; they felt that she had no business to be there. Moreover, it was almost a slur on them, if she was there. There was something obscurely wrong about it ; the idea offended them. It hurt their pride. It went against their deep, unconscious notions of what was right and proper. All this was, at bottom, a matter of feeling, not of thinking. It had very little to do with the facts of working life, at any time. Workers who spoke and thought thus were, in so doing, departing from experience ; they were not thinking with their own minds. They were, without knowing it, taking over the thinking of the small leisured class. In that class there was, once, a creature called the " lady ", a delicate, fragile being, who fainted at the sight of blood, and must be sheltered by her masculine protector from the harsh facts of common life. Of this being, the proper sphere was the drawing-room ; the room withdrawn from the struggle and the stress. This picture was long used to keep the middle-class girl in helpless ignorance, and, often, to condemn her, if she remained single, as many did, to misery and want in her later years. Never at any time did it fit the circumstances or the actual living conditions of the great body of women ; least of all did it fit the women of the working class. Working-class women, whether they work at home or outside it, are, of course, the vast majority of their sex. At no time have they been "sheltered". They have, however, been weakened, and that seriously, in their exposed struggle to make ends meet by notions that have never in the least fitted their case, or expressed the realities of their lives. The " ladies " have never been more than a handful. The rest of womenkind have always, like their men-folk, worked because they had to.

Women at Work

Outside the home, and in it, the ordinary woman pays her way by work. Yet the theory that every woman lives, not by her own work, but by the work of some man, dies hard. It has had, and still has, a profound and far-reaching effect. It gravely increases the difficulties daily met by women at work, whatever the work may be.

This old view ought to have vanished with the political emancipation of women in 1919. But it has by no means wholly vanished yet. It is, however, far less widespread than it was before the 1914–18 war. The process has been slow and gradual by which the outlook of women about themselves and, as a consequence, that of men about them, has changed. The long struggle for female education, for admission to the professions, for civic rights, which makes one of the most significant chapters in the history of the later half of the nineteenth century, had its effect ; thinking women began to use their own minds on this major question of democracy —their own equality. The effect of this carried over into all other spheres. It carried over very notably into the thinking of Trade Unionists. The gallant efforts of the Women's Trade Union League—to be more fully described later—bore fruit in steady conversion. Moreover, the general attitude of the Unions was affected and that deeply by the rise, in the '90's, of the great general labour Unions, and the appearance of Unions of " black-coats ". These new general Unions sought to gather in all the workers ; they also fixed their standard contribution fairly low. In this their policy differed widely from that of the older craft Unions which maintained a high standard both of contribution and of technical efficiency in their membership—a point on which they resemble closely the strictly professional associations of doctors, architects, feachers, etc. The strength of the craft Union lay in the approved and hall-marked competence of its members. The strength of new Unions, like the Dockers, Gas Workers and General Labourers, depended on the comprehensiveness of their intake. Naturally, therefore, they were sympathetic to women ; they also saw, more clearly than many of the older Unions, how dangerous it was to keep them out. Even to-day, a few craft Unions bar women from membership, but the lead given by the Textile Unions has been followed by Unions like the Transport and General Workers and the Municipal and General Workers and the Distributive Workers in efforts to bring them in. To-day the official policy of the Trade Union Movement is directed, strongly and clearly, to the fullest inclusion of women. Thus, speaking as chairman at the 1937 conference at Norwich, Mr. Ernest Bevin said :

> The position of women in industry creates a tremendous problem for this Movement. It will never be solved until we can get a common acceptance by the male section in Congress that in every industry it is the common duty of men and women alike to be organised in Trade Unions. We have made some progress, but only the fringe of the problem has as yet been touched. The wages of women, having regard to the value of the work they perform, are far too low, and tend to keep down the general level of wages.

It will be part of the task of these pages to trace the stages by which the men's Unions were converted. Meantime, the statement of this notion of organisation as a duty, incumbent on man and woman, marks a stage in the evolution of the Trade Union idea, and a very significant one. It represents what may be called the positive, as against the negative side of Trade Unionism. The negative side is, and remains, important. From this angle, Trade Unionism is a system of protection : a means whereby the strength of associated numbers is used to meet and offset the strength of money. The labour of one worker can be done without ; the labour of all workers cannot be done without. When the many stand behind the one, he can resist injustice. Mary Macarthur, who put so many things well in her day, used to tell a story that admirably sums up this aspect, in terms as simple as they are realistic :

" You have all heard of the foolish old woman who went out and bought a bundle of sticks tied tightly together with a piece of string. She was in a hurry to get the fire lit when she came home, so she tried to break the bundle as it was. What was the result ? She did not break the sticks. She nearly broke her fingers instead. Had she untied the string, each stick could easily have been broken separately, but united together the sticks protected each other, and could not be broken.

" A Trade Union is like a bundle of sticks. The workers are bound together and have the strength of unity. No employer can do as he likes with them. They have the power of resistance. They can ask for an advance without fear. A worker who is not in a Union is like a single stick. She can easily be broken or bent to the will of her employer. She has no power to resist a reduction in wages. If she is fined, she must pay without complaint. She dare not ask for a ' rise '. If she does, she will be told ' Your place is outside the gates ; there are plenty to take your place.'

" An employer can do without one worker. He cannot do without all his workers. If all the workers united in a Union—strong as the bundle of sticks—complain, or ask for improved conditions, the employer is bound to listen."

The fair-minded employer to-day realises the advantage, for himself, of dealing, through recognised machinery, with the difficulties that arise in work, and settling them by discussion and negotiation. The right to strike—to withhold labour—remains, as the background strength of the united workers ; but it is rather by the opportunity given by the Union's existence of stating a fair case, than by the use of the strike, that workers have actually won improved conditions and a new status. Through Trade Union action, in nine cases out of ten, reason and argument replace force ; and open negotiation, between men who can trust in one another's pledged word, affords to millions of workers a real safeguard against injustice.

The positive side of Trade Unionism, however, is even more important. In a Trade Union, persons come together freely for mutual aid. The word " mutual ", here, is as significant as is the word " free ", and the two are inescapably tied together : the one cannot exist without the other. Real freedom, like real fullness of life, can only be compassed when individuals frankly recognise the basic fact that the existence of others conditions theirs at every turn. When entrenched power denies the right of free association for mutual aid it wilfully stunts the growth of man and denies his most vital means to freedom ; more than that, it violates a quite fundamental human instinct. That we live, and can only live, together, and not in isolation, is an elementary fact ; the instinct that prompts men to associate and help one another is not less primary than the selfish and self-regarding instinct ; moreover, it is fruitful, whereas the other is sterile. In strengthening association among workers, Trade Union- ism has served not its own members only : it has served and is serving the community. Association fortifies the whole personality of the man or woman who enters into it ; it releases capacities that could not function in solitude. The life of a free community demands that its members should recognise constantly and respect sympathetically their inalterable interdependence. For every conscious Trade Unionist, this is a real fact.

Nor is this all. Modern conditions of work have taken much away that the craftsman of earlier times enjoyed. He cannot savour in any fullness the joy of creation. Much of the world's necessary work is drudgery, in itself uninteresting. The worker of to-day seldom makes more than a part, and generally a very small and, in itself, unmeaning part, of anything. This is his fate whether he be called a worker by hand or a worker by brain. This loss is part of the price that has to be paid for large-scale production : for the service of the machine. It brings a loss to the worker. Yet it also brings its curious compensation. He has to know, from direct and repeated experience in his daily task, that without his fellows he is nothing and can make nothing ; with them, he is capable of being and making anything. The vast ship, the complicated machine, the published book, the intricate machinery of lighting, feeding, and draining a vast city—all these are accomplished by an elaborate co-operation, in which the part of each is at once indispensable and at the same time unmeaning without the part of the others. So, the worker is freed from the illusion of being in his own person self-contained and self-sufficient. He knows that his existence depends upon and is part of the existence of others ; he knows that full self-expression can only be realised in co-operation with them.

Moreover, the worker who works in association with his fellows, who feels his cause is theirs, who is ready to risk present safety to prevent injustice, knows something of enormous moral import about work itself. He knows that it is not a curse, but at once the duty and the dignity of the citizen. The worker gives to, as well as takes from, the common stock. The idler fails in this primary obligation. The exploiter of others sins against it. To the labourer worthy of his hire there belongs a rightful pride. He may not get his due, but he gives it. This pride is warmed to something nobler by the sense of comradeship. Here is perhaps the most precious aspect of association. Knowledge of personal worth is lifted by Trade Union membership into an awareness of social worth which breeds a genuine loyalty to the fellows with whom a man's own work is tied up.

Does this seem a somewhat romantic account of the positive aspect of Trade Unionism ?—something far from the thoughts of the average member who, somewhat grudgingly, pays his dues, seldom attends a Branch meeting, and criticises his leaders without much sympathy ? Granted, it is not the aspect of Trade Unionism about which actual Trade Unionists talk much. Nevertheless, they feel it ; here is the vision and the truth that has fed the steady growth of the movement and carried it, steadily and surely, through every kind of difficulty and over all sorts of obstacles, to ever-increasing strength and self-confidence, as it has kept its servants faithful, alert, devoted, careless of personal reward and constantly ready to risk everything for a cause. No one, certainly, who remembers 1926, and the selfless devotion of the men and women who came out in support of the miners regardless of the risks to themselves, can doubt that interdependence among workers is a fact, and no cold fact ; or doubt that the comradeship of the Union is an element of enrichment in their lives and lasting value in that of the community. Aspects of 1926 there are which are best buried and forgotten ; but the superb loyalty of the workers is something that it warms the heart to have known and to remember.

Moreover, the Trade Unionist knows that he belongs to a great fellowship whose boundaries are wider than those of his own employment or even of his own country.

Every year since 1868, representatives of a widening band of Unions have met together in annual congress to discuss matters that concern them as workers ; except when interrupted by war, fraternal delegates from all parts of the world have joined them there, to meet as friends and exchange experiences and counsels. In times of stress, the workers of Britain have again and again generously helped their comrades overseas ; to-day, in war, the knowledge of what their brothers are enduring under the Nazi heel never leaves them : rather it adds a tinge of passion to their determination to keep and to extend their own associations. This yearly parliament is a great democratic assembly, at once realistic and tolerant ; minorities as well as majorities make their views heard. The debates contribute to the forming of national public opinion and affect national action. Congress elects a Council, to carry on the affairs of the united Movement from day to day, assisted, at Headquarters (Transport House), by a fine staff of expert workers, headed by a Secretary, Sir Walter Citrine, who is recognised, on performance, as a statesman of no mean order. In Congress, women delegates, who appeared as delegates in Congress as early as 1874, are on an equality with men in all but numbers ; a woman (Margaret Bondfield) has presided over Congress[1] ; two places for women are reserved on the General Council.

Loyalty and comradeship, like the lift given by association to daily action and daily endurance through their connexion with a great idea, are precious gains that Trade Unionism can bring to women. To them, perhaps, they are even more important than to men. In work, they carry certain disabilities. They are rated—and still tend to rate themselves—as secondary beings. This is a hang-over from a long past ; it cannot easily or swiftly be cast off ; although it is being cast off by many. They are assumed—without much solid ground—to have a lower living standard. They are assumed—with even less ground—to have nobody to keep but themselves. They are regarded, in many cases, as " transients " in industry, who will go out, when they marry, although they may have to come back again later, either freely or under the stern compulsion of immediate need, when hardship, for one reason or another, strikes the home. Because of their transience, they are often not taken seriously as workers (least of all when promotion is in question) either by their colleagues, their employers, or themselves.

---

[1] Margaret Bondfield was chairman of the General Council in 1923-4, but did not preside at Congress owing to her entry into the 1924 Labour Government.

All these disabilities are real, and have their effect. More serious than any of them is the fact that a very large proportion of working women work, not in factories, in close association with their fellows, but in small groups, or even singly. This is the case both with the large numbers engaged in personal service, and in commerce. For hundreds of thousands, both the sense and the fact of isolation aggravate difficulties and disabilities. Women workers, even more than men, need the support and the strength that association brings. They need it, first, in their wages and their working conditions. There is, for instance, no solution of the problem of female underpayment except the establishment of a Trade Union rate for the job. There is no hope that women workers will achieve economic equality, inside or outside industry, except through action taken in connexion with men, and based on their whole-hearted co-operation. The Trade Union is the vanguard, here, of the entire movement for the full achievement of democracy. Freedom and self-respect in work with the right to choose and put a point of view, and to win agreement for it through argument and discussion—these are the basic claims of Trade Unionism. It fights, as it has always fought, for decent pay and decent conditions for the workers, because without these things they cannot be wholly free to think their own thoughts and live their own lives in their own way. Yet, through all the incidents of the day-to-day struggle for fair material conditions, there moves the knowledge that this fight is but an incident in the fight for human freedom. Without the workers, the life of the community could not go on for a day. Trade Unionism asserts therefore the right to have a view and to put it, about the manner in which the community's life is organised, and should and could be organised. Inevitably, Trade Unions are in politics ; more, they stand for the social transformation which will make the machine man's servant, instead of being, as now, his master ; and will complete political freedom by bringing about the social and economic freedom which will make democracy a reality.

These things are part of the woman's charter, as they are of the man's. But while these larger purposes of the Trade Union movement appeal, and that strongly, to women, and while its protective action and activity are essential to them, there is another aspect that is, for them, exceptionally important.

This is its contribution to their personal lives. Trade Union membership can help, and that potently, to rid women of the painful sense of being inferior creatures which has been bred in them by decades of practical subjection and imputed worthlessness. The dead oppression and the consequent weakness, born of this continual assumption that what a woman is or does does not matter ; that she is, by a doom which no action of her own can alter, destined always to inferiority of performance and status : these things are hard for men to understand. They lie like a pall of lead over the efforts of women. Here is, in fact, by far the most heavy and painful of their imposed disabilities. They do not expect to succeed ; they do not expect to be decently paid ; they take it for granted that they are beasts of burden. Resistance, struggle, initiative, are hard for them, just because the conventional picture does not allow them any of these attributes, and because they are so often condemned to solitude in their effort and in their toil.

Here, the Union can do a vast deal for them. They

take to the experience of solidarity with touching eagerness, once they are given a taste of it ; their loyalty is, admittedly, unfaltering, once it is called upon. Inside the Union, they are no longer inferiors. They are members, like other members. That is all, and all-sufficient. They are no longer isolated ; they become part of a band.

Moreover, through companionship in work, there comes to them the pride in work itself that lifts the head and carries the mind cheerfully through inevitable drudgery. Once they are joined members of a Union, the invigorating influence of the force of association makes itself felt ; steady loyalty and firmness can be counted on from women members. Proof, here, of how much they profit by the change-over from loneliness to association.

To-day, the vast majority of Unions admit women to membership, and, once they are in, treat them on an equality. There still persists a custom under which the woman's contribution (assessed on the basis of her lower wages) is lower than the man's ; in some, too, this lower contribution carries a discrimination ; it cannot be said that, as yet, the woman's share of executive and administrative responsibility is anything like level with her membership. Few are the Unions which expect their women members to share in the leadership of the Union, although all expect—and get —a very high standard of followership from them. Here, however, the ball is at the women's feet.

It may be urged that the obstacle to Trade Unionism among women—and, of course, the rate of unionisation is deplorably low—is the very fact that constitutes their greatest need of it—the isolated, irregular, and ill-paid nature of much of their work. To the factory worker, the appeal of the Union is near and intelligible without much argument upon the matter. But the domestic servant, like the charwoman, the odd " help ", or even the clerk, is in a different case. They have no easy or direct contact either with other workers, or with the organisations that speak for workers. Again, many women work under circumstances that militate directly against joining a Union ; this is the case with the shop assistants, the typists, and again, the domestic workers, who, continually in contact with members of a higher social class, are tempted to admire their ways and habits and seek rather to be like them than to associate with other workers.

All this is true. It is, with the youth, the transience, and the economic weakness of women, the main explanation of their relatively low Trade Union proportion. It remains a fact that the very severity of women's need for organisation to protect them is the major obstacle to their organisation. But, in this, women are not peculiar. The case of large numbers of working men is the same ; the same, with the single exception of the transience of women in paid employment. To the women who regard work as merely a stage in their life, and therefore feel no call to " do anything about it ", even for their own advantage, the words of J. R. Clynes may well be quoted, for they have a lasting relevance and truth :

> Many women naturally look upon their employment in factory or workshop as a temporary stage in their life. It may be temporary for the individual, but it is permanent for the class. Women who do not join a Trade Union tend not only to keep down their own level, but also to lower the level for men workers, and also lower the level of their own sisters or that of the men-folk in their homes.

This is the decisive point. Trade Union action, in securing a decent level of wages and conditions, tends to the benefit of all who work and all who depend upon work. It is, that is to say, as much for the benefit of the home-keeping woman as for her sister who " goes out " to office, service, factory or shop. Nor do its benefits end here. It brings into the lives of all concerned with it the sense of comradeship, and the knowledge that, together, they are concerned in something larger and more lasting than their individual selves.

CHAPTER III

ORGANISATION AS IT IS TO-DAY

WHEN one turns to ask how far are women organised, as workers, the answer is, at first, disappointing. One occupied man in every three belongs to some kind of Trade Union. Of women returned by the 1931 Census as occupied, only 552,585 were then in Unions affiliated with the Trades Union Congress, together with some 160,000 Teachers and 55,000 Civil Servants, organised in non-affiliated Unions.[1]

It is true that in recent years, the *rate* of unionisation for women increased faster than has the rate for men : as has the rate of employment. In 1933 one woman in every seven was in a Union. Yet the discrepancy remains. It justifies to the hilt the statement by Ernest Bevin that " Only the fringe of the problem has, as yet, been touched ". So long as six women out of every seven employed are unorganised, the six will tend to drag down and depress the prospects and opportunities not only of the seven, but of the men associated with them in the occupations where they work.

The broad general figures do not, however, tell one much about the actual position. They need to be broken up, before that can emerge.

When that is done it appears that what may be called " the incidence of unionisation " is very irregular, both in the case of women and of men ; for both, there are great groups hardly touched. In the great productive

[1] Trade Union membership figures are throughout those for 1939, the nearest normal year.

and distributive industries, and above all in what the Census calls " factory employment ", the rate is relatively high. It is higher for men ; but it is also high for women.

But, out of the $5\frac{1}{2}$ million odd women employed, only over a million and three-quarters (1,855,586) are in factory employment.

Nor is this all. A high proportion of the women in factory employment are in a very small number of industrial groups—textiles, clothing, boot and shoe, printing and paper, pottery, metal trades, and employment in shops and minor factory industries taking the bulk of them.

Thus, out of the 552,585 women in Unions affiliated to the Trades Union Congress, no fewer than 428,000 are covered by 10 Unions :

Weavers' Association	70,736
Tailors and Garment Workers	66,607
Distributive and Allied Workers	54,117
General and Municipal Workers	43,321
Cardroom Amalgamation	36,776
Dyers	35,972
Transport and General Workers	33,481
Boot and Shoe	34,905
Printing and Bookbinding	31,000
Shop Assistants	25,514
Pottery Workers	14,292
Hosiery	11,797

Even this list hardly does justice to the actual concentration of Union membership. Out of the 428,000 comprised in the 12 Unions listed above, nearly 143,000 are in the three Unions covering the Textile trades, since the Dyers take in most of the organised women in the woollen and worsted branches of the Textiles. If Hosiery with its 11,800, be added, the Textile total becomes 155,000—well over a quarter of the entire number of women in Unions of any sort.

In the Textiles as a whole, as in its separate sections—weaving, spinning, clothing and hosiery—the women employed greatly outnumber the men. Thus, the great block of unionised women are in Unions that cover a distinct, though very important section of industry : distinct in place, in that it is concentrated in certain well-defined areas ; and distinct in character, in that, in it, women workers are in a numerical majority. This separateness of the Textiles will have to be examined in more detail later.

Next in unionised numbers to the Textiles come the Distributive trades, which cover shops, stores and warehouses of all kinds, including the stores belonging to the Co-operative Societies. Here women form a large but not preponderating part of the total body of workers. They are working often, but not always, side by side with men. Between them the National Union of Distributive and Allied Workers and the National Union of Shop Assistants cover over 80,000 women members.

Not far behind the Distributives come the great bodies of miscellaneous workers, including workers in the metal and minor metal and engineering trades, and in factories of various kinds, covered by the General and Municipal Workers (over 43,000) and the Transport and General Workers (35,000). For the women called in, under stress of war, to make munitions and to fill the places of men with the colours, these two Unions are the primary spokesmen ; and most gallantly and successfully have they risen to the huge task thus imposed upon them. In these two very large and powerful Unions women are, of course, in normal times, in a small minority ; nevertheless the entire weight of their powerful membership has been thrown behind the claim for a fair deal for the woman war worker.

Proportionately to total numbers, women are very important in the Boot and Shoe Trades (31,000 members of the Union being women and 56,000 men) ; they also enjoy an unusual measure of equality of treatment in that industry.

Printing and Bookbinding are among the skilled trades in which women have played a part from the first. There are only 6,000 odd women to 21,000 men in the National Society of Operative Printers ; but in the larger National Union of Printing, Bookbinding and Paper Workers there are 31,000 women members, against 40,000 men.

This brief list covers the large groups of organised women, and shows their high concentration in a few groups. Fourteen thousand Pottery workers, and just under 12,000 Hosiery workers, complete the list of large groups. True, teachers and civil servants and one big Union of Local Government Officers are not affiliated to Congress, although unionised ; and nurses are hardly unionised at all.

Yet even when these are added, two facts stand out : (*a*) the majority of women workers are in a small number of Unions (and of industrial groups), and (*b*) small, often very small blocks of women appear over a very wide range of employment. The appendix to this chapter is well worth attentive study.

It shows that women do not appear at all in certain major industries where Trade Unionism has long history, and is very strong. Thus group 1, Mining and Quarrying, contains over 600,000 men, and no women.[1] Group 4, Shipbuilding, has 83,950 men, and no women. In Group 5, the largest unit, the Amalgamated Engineering Union, with 333,619 members, excludes women. In Group 6, Compositors, Electrotypers and Lithographers, also bar their doors. Even in Textiles (9) women are not admitted as Overlookers or Spinners. For one reason and another, Unions in a series of groups which represent great strength in the Trade Union structure include no women.

On the other hand, very large numbers of women are in occupations in which organisation is weak among men. This is a cardinal point. It is often forgotten, but it never ought to be forgotten.

Even the slightest and most general sketch map of women's work indeed reveals this as a leading feature of their place in the world of organised labour. True, they are, as workers, predominantly young—and therefore inapt for organisation. True they are also predominantly in and out of paid work—and, again, thereby inapt for organisation. But an even more significant fact about them is shown by any enumeration of main categories in which their employment falls. They belong, in the main, to precisely those groups of employment in which organisation has always proved most difficult, whether of women or of men : the ill-paid, irregular, casual and isolated kinds of work.

It is with this fact in mind that the figures of Trade Union membership must be read, if they are to be appreciated. It is with this fact in mind that the statement so often made, that " Women are difficult to organise " must be taken, and by this weighted.

[1] Women have of course been excluded by law from working underground since 1842.

Look at the actual main categories of female employment, as given by the Census.

The largest block—larger than factory employment —is Personal Service, with close on 2 millions. To the organiser, this category has always presented enormous difficulties. They have not been surmounted in the case of the men in a branch of personal service less intractable than that domestic one which takes so many women—Hotel and Restaurant service.

Next comes " Commercial and Clerical Employment ", which occupies another million and a quarter. Here, for the organiser of men, is another hard nut to crack—and one which is not cracked in their case.

The difficulties, here, are of the same nature as in the personal service category, in so far as the worker is as a rule isolated and the character of the work, and its associations, are such as militate against the Trade Union appeal.

The other big block speaks for itself. It is casual and intermittent employment. No argument needed to stress the point that the casual worker, man or woman, is hard to get at and harder still to hold.

Does it not look as though any general statement about difficulty of organising women, as women, had as slender a basis as does duty for most of the generalisations allowed to pass current when made about one-half of the human race, which would be laughed at if attempted about the other ?

In the very useful volume on British Trade Unionism, published in 1939, G. D. H. Cole, as editor, writes a chapter on what he calls " Strength and Weakness in British Trade Unionism ". It is illuminating, in more ways than one ; and highly relevant here. Mr. Cole states :

" There are certain very large classes of persons whom Trade Unionism has touched either not at all or to a negligible extent." He cites five great groups, as being in this position. He lists them as—

(1) Domestic workers ;
(2) Clerks and Typists ;
(3) Workers on the Land ;
(4) Unskilled and Casual Workers ;
(5) Women.

No quarrel possible with this list, except in so far as it gives women as a separate category, whereas they are already in fact covered under heads (1), (2) and (4).

(1), (2) and (4) include nearly all the women not comprised under factory employment or professional employment. These three groups, with (3) land-workers, cover between them the persons, male or female, who are hard to organise because of the very conditions of their employment. To make of women another group is to count the same persons twice over. Here is an example of the way in which, even by the clearest and most instructed minds, logic is apt to be abandoned where women are concerned. In fact, difficulty of organisation is a function of the type of work, not of the sex of the worker.

This fact needs to be stressed, since it explains many puzzles about the employment of women. They are, in the main, employed under conditions, and on terms, that give them a weak bargaining position, and make it exceptionally hard for them to achieve the protection of organisation, gravely as they need it. They are, as casual, unskilled and domestic workers, scattered. They are, on the whole, very poorly paid. The conditions of their work are isolated ; they are conditions unfavourable, from that angle, as from others, to the Trade Union appeal. Yet such workers need, desperately, the support which only association can give.

Recall, once more, that out of the 5½ million women employed, nearly 2 million are in " personal service "— i.e. domestic work and (domestic) charing, in the main ; another million are in clerical and commercial employment—that is, the clerks and typists of Mr. Cole's group.   More than half of the women employed, that is to say, are in the groups which Trade Unionism has not touched at all, or only to a negligible extent.   Less than a third of occupied women are in the category described by the Census as Factory Employment.   Yet the strength of Trade Unionism, among men, is, of course, here : it is also here among women.   The percentage of organisation among women is pulled down to a very low level largely by the fact that the task of the organiser of women has got to be, in the main, that of organising scattered and often isolated domestic, clerical, commercial and casual workers, since it is among them that the bulk of women workers are found.   Where workers are gathered together in a factory, there is a keen and natural sense of common interest and common concern.   There, organisation arises out of the conditions of day-to-day association in work itself.   It is then obvious that a grievance felt by one can affect all, and be the concern of all.   It is then obvious that each has a duty and an interest in helping the other.   There can be talk about details of work and common action to put right anything that is plainly unjust or unfair.   Once this common action has been effectively tried, it acts as a stimulus to the next essay ; a sense of strength is born of the realised fact of unity.

Organisation as it is To-day

Very different is the case of the isolated worker. Her—or his—need of the support of fellowship is as great ; nay, far greater. Yet it is hard to get at her ; hard to bring her into the association through which she could help herself ; easy for her to slip out, even if on some sudden impulse she has been moved to join. Her employer treats her as a unit, readily replaceable by someone more " reliable " if she makes any complaint, however just, and tries to stand up for her own rights or those of another. There is none of the exhilaration of corporate work to lift her out of the slough of despond ; she is easily " put upon ", and easily made to feel she does not matter. These are the workers who need Trade Unionism most, not only in their working conditions, but in their daily life, which is apt to be bleak of companionship. At the same time, they present the Trade Union organiser with hard problems. It is not to be wondered at if, occasionally, on some brief suspension of loyal and devoted work he—and even she—subscribes to the doctrine that " Women are hard to organise ", and relapses into the belief that there is something in the sex, over and above any conditions and circumstances, that accounts for the relatively low proportion of organised women.

Whether there really is anything in a view which ascribes to women in this connexion an extra dose of original sin cannot be determined until conditions in some at any rate of the employments in which women appear in large numbers have been inspected rather more closely. Even before doing that, however, it will be well to review the steady and devoted efforts that have been made, notably in the last fifty years, to promote organisation and overcome prejudice—prejudice on the part of employers, of fellow workers, and of women themselves. For this, a long line of men and women work and have worked, in season and out of season, selflessly and tirelessly ; many of them un- known save in their own localities and in their own industries, seeking no reward beyond the sense that they have brought help and hope to those who need it sorely ; fighting the battle of women workers, which is, at the same time, the battle of men. Some of the fighters of the past must be recorded, although many more have to be left out.

(See Appendix, Women in the Principal Unions at the end of the book.)

CHAPTER IV

THE WOMEN'S TRADE UNION LEAGUE

I

LONDONERS who happened to be out of doors on any of the streets that lead from Mile End to Fleet Street on a certain very hot afternoon in July 1888 saw a sight that made many of them stop and stare. Along the streets some hundreds of working girls were pouring along in quick irregular march. They were obviously in a high state of excitement. They talked, as they streamed along; from time to time, they sang; then again, they would fall quite silent, with grave, even solemn expressions on their youthful faces. On they came like a river in flood. Policeman stared, but let them pass; they were orderly enough, though unfamiliar. Plainly this was no planned or formal march; some sudden and strong impulse had set them in motion; they were going somewhere. Hatless, and mostly very young—ages from fourteen to sixteen or seventeen, they wore the long skirts of the day, bunched up at the back and joined to tight bodices fitting high to the throat. Their thin and rather shabby shoes were not in the least intended for long walks. In most cases their hair was gathered up in a tight bun at the back, and cut over the eyes in a deep fringe. Their speech showed that they were working girls; girls from some East End factory.

They were. They were girls from the big match

factory of Messrs. Bryant & May. There, for fourteen hours a day they worked ; at the end of a week the wage most of them brought home was well under eight shillings and in many cases as small as four shillings and tenpence. It had never occurred to most of them that they could expect anything different. The other day, however, a wonderful and lovely woman had suddenly appeared in the factory. She was friendly ; she had the most marvellous great grey eyes ; her voice was soft and yet thrillingly warm ; she had talked to the girls. They had told about their work and their pay ; and her eyes had flashed ; she had said it was abominable. She went away. Next day, the forewoman gave notice to the girls who had dared to talk. They were dismissed, on the spot. They had said nothing that was not true. The injustice of their dismissal roused the others. A wave of hot indignation passed from girl to girl, as the news reached them. Before, they had never dared resist anything that was put upon them. Now, however, perhaps as the result of the sympathy shown them by their wonderful visitor ; perhaps because this victimisation was the last straw that makes the worm turn, they were roused. " Why don't we all of us just walk out on them ? " asked a bold spirit. At once, her words were taken up enthusiastic- ally. In vain, the representatives of the manage- ment argued and threatened. Walk out they did, all of them. Within minutes, they were in the street.

Once outside the factory gates, there was a bad moment of cold fear. What were they to do now ? What was going to happen to them ? They would all lose their jobs ; that was certain, and nothing else was. But soon the stronger spirits rallied the weaker. They

were " for it " now ; there could be no going back.   As
to what they were to do, that was easy ; they must at
once consult the wonderful woman who had shown
such interest in them the other day.   She would tell
them.   Off therefore they pelted to the Fleet Street
office of a little weekly paper called *The Link.*

The Link—in other words the torch—had been started
not so very long before by Mrs. Annie Besant, for the
express purpose of throwing light in dark places ; showing up abuses ; waking Londoners to realising what
London was like for many of its citizens.   *The Link* ran
a feature called The Pillory to expose bad conditions of
employment.   Herbert Burrows, an ardent Socialist,
told her that truly shocking conditions existed in the
East London match factories ; he took her down to
Bryant & Mays.   After what she saw, she wrote a
fiery article, which caused all the trouble.

Now she was sitting at her table, writing another
flaming piece, when she heard the noise of many
feet on the narrow stairs ; within moments, her room,
and the staircase leading up to it, and the street below
was packed with girls, all talking at once.   It took a
minute before she could get a straight story out of them.
When she did, and she understood what had happened,
her eyes flashed.   They had, she assured them, done
quite right to walk out ; that was a grand action.
They must now stay out, and not let anybody get into
the factory.   The firm, the girls told her, threatened to
import workers ; or even to transfer the factory to
Norway.   She laughed ; they could not do that.   If
the girls stood fast, they would be all right.   She had
friends, who would be friends of theirs and would help
them ; she would collect money for them ; she would
make London ring with their story.   All they had got

to do was to stand firm. " Don't let anybody frighten you," she urged. " We will look after you." Meantime, they must do everything in orderly fashion. They must choose a committee from among themselves, to manage things ; they must picket the factory ; above all they must keep their heads and not get panicky. The girls listened, thrilled ; the courage that had inspired them to walk out burned high ; they pledged themselves, one and all, to do as she said. They had complete confidence in her.

She was as good as her word. Before the week was out, she called all the girls together for a great mass meeting ; there, the first instalment of strike pay was handed out to them. Annie Besant was there and Herbert Burrows, Bernard Shaw and Graham Wallas. The two latter carried a great bag containing five hundred pounds in coin ; this was poured out on to the table, and counted out ; then the girls filed by one by one to get their pay handed to them by Mrs. Besant. To her the girls looked up, almost with worship ; they crowded round to kiss her skirts ; for them, she seemed little short of an angel.

She meantime had taken up her pen, to good effect ; and got others to take theirs with letters and articles in the papers. She had got a grand story, and she knew it. She also knew how to tell it. The public, moreover, was ready to respond. Especially in London, there was at this time a great stir going out about working conditions. Revelations by the Salvation Army and by Charles Booth and others had stirred many consciences ; there was a lot of feeling about the unemployed ; the Socialist movement was beginning. When people read the story of conditions in Bryant & May's they were horrified ; young girls toiling fourteen hours a day for a wage of five shillings was more than they could comfortably contemplate. It made matters worse to be reminded that Bryant & May's had, not so very long ago, put up a statue to Mr. Gladstone and levied every girl in their employ one shilling to help to pay for it ; or that their latest dividend was 22 per cent. In most quarters there was recognition of the courage shown by the girls in coming out in defence of companions whom the firm had treated with sheer indefensible tyranny ; there was also an outraged sympathy with their miserable conditions. True, *The Times* was very solemn about the wickedness of strikes ; talked heavily about the " class war " ; and muttered that all the trouble was due to the evil Socialists. Other newspapers, however, ardently took up the girls' cause ; the match girls were almost heroines. All sorts of people came down to help. Herbert Burrows got the girls to form a Union, of which he acted as honorary secretary. Stewart Headlam and Sydney Olivier joined the other Fabian leaders in helping.

What settled the issue, however, was the grand courage and firmness of the girls themselves ; and the help that came to them from organised Labour in London. The London Trades Council, representing all the men's Unions in the metropolis, came out strongly in support of the strike. The Women's Trade Union League collected money for the strike fund ; they raised four hundred pounds in less than a week ; it also sent down a corps of organisers to Mile End, who helped to form the Union and to hold it together. On this the girls were very keen, at the time ; in their ranks there was no break ; many of them, indeed, thoroughly enjoyed the adventure. Very soon, the firm realised that they had got against them a force too strong to disregard ;

they actually agreed to recognise the Union of Match-makers, and to negotiate a settlement with it. In fact, at the end of three weeks, a settlement was reached. It gave the girls fair conditions and decent wages, and took them all back. From 1888 on, indeed, Bryant & May's has been recognised as something of a model factory.

It is true that the Match Girls' Union did not live very long ; by 1903 it winked out, like so many other societies started with high hopes in a burst of strong enthusiasm stimulated by some outstanding grievance. But they had accomplished something that did last, something that had most important consequences ; something that entitled them to a lasting and honour-able place in any history of Trade Unionism. " The match girls' victory turned a new leaf in Trade Union annals. Hitherto, success had been in almost exact proportion to the workers' strength. It was a new experience to have the weak succeed because of their very weakness, by means of the intervention of the public." This is the verdict of Sidney and Beatrice Webb, in their great *History of Trade Unionism*, first published in 1894. They go on to say : " The lesson was not lost." In fact the success of the match girls was like a beacon light held up to other unskilled and underpaid workers. It set going a great stirring in the whole of London's East End. If girls, wretchedly paid and socially and economically as weak a group of workers as could anywhere be found, could bring a powerful employer to his knees within three weeks, why could not men do the same ? A direct result of the example of the match girls was the uprising among the gas workers. Under Will Thorne and Ben Tillett they, in the spring of 1889, formed a Union which rapidly enrolled workers by the thousand ; and in August 1889 demanded a reduction of their hours of labour from twelve to eight. To the surprise of the men no less than of the public, this was granted. The dockers came next. For years Ben Tillett, then a labourer in one of the great tea houses, had been struggling to get his mates to form a Union. In August 1889, there was a sudden downing of tools on a demand for sixpence per hour on the part of a group of men working in the South West India Dock. Tillett called on John Burns and Tom Mann to come down and help ; the call went out to dock labourers as a body ; and as a body they rose in response. Within three days 10,000 labourers had left work ; the Craft Unions joined forces ; John Burns filled the entire body with strong and disciplined enthusiasm. Once again, the public was roused ; the call for the " dockers' tanner " created a powerful wave of sympathy, and a great flow of funds from all sections and even from distant Australia, which remitted over thirty thousand pounds to London by telegraph. Arbitration was accepted ; the men got practically all they had come out for. Beyond and above that was the firm establishment of a series of strong Unions of general labourers. This great result, which has revolutionised both conditions of work and the Trade Union movement itself, was in large measure rendered possible by the demonstration afforded by the helpless match girls.

Annie Besant herself moved on to other fields of work. There have, in the movement for the industrial as for the social emancipation of women, always been people like her who contribute something, but whose enthusiasm, however ardent and sincere, is not lasting in its direction. Side by side with them, however, and

47

more lastingly important, are the people whose names are not often known, but whose enthusiasm is steady and durable. There has never been a time, from the days of the early struggles against terrible conditions in the new factories and workplaces of the early nineteenth century down to the present day, when numbers of women have not played a staunch and faithful part in the fight against injustice whether to their fellow-women or to their fellow-men, and faithfully stuck to it, day in, day out, doing for its sake hard and dull work, lit by no hope of personal recognition. A great many of these true heroines of the working women's movement are unknown outside a narrow circle ; unknown in the past, as they are to-day in the present, except to those whom they helped and inspired. Yet a movement which has already many splendid names has been made possible and now goes on because of the unwearied and tenacious devotion of countless helpers and servers, up and down the country, who ask no other reward than the sense that they are carrying forward a cause in which they believe. It is the unnamed who have made the whole thing possible. It is the unnamed who carry the main burden, still. The qualities of leadership were never lacking. Anyone who studies the annals of the working-class movement in the last two decades of the nineteenth century and the first quarter of the twentieth century in particular, must be struck by the very notable band of women who worked, sometimes separately, often together, and always in effective, disinterested and un-self-seeking devotion to a common cause. Most of them were not what are called " feminists ", though the feminists also played their part. They worked, it is true, primarily for women —for the simple reason that women had the greatest need of their help. Always, however, they had before them a big general human purpose. They came into line with the feminists in so far as they asserted, first on this line and then on that, that women were human beings, and should be treated by the community as human beings equally with men. At the same time, that was a revolutionary point of view.

On the political side, the drive came mainly from the women of the Independent Labour Party, since that party was ahead of the Trade Union side of the Labour movement in making the equality of women an effective plank in its social programme. It gave pioneers like Enid Stacey and Caroline Martin and Katherine Bruce Glasier—the last a figure of wonderful gallantry, courage and faithfulness, for whom time, loss, disappointment, brought no weariness and no relaxation of effort or enthusiasm for the cause. To the I L P, Margaret Bondfield, Mary Macarthur and Margaret MacDonald also belonged ; they functioned both on the political and on the industrial side, as did later Susan Lawrence and Ellen Wilkinson ; Marion Phillips was mainly active on the political side ; Julia Varley and Gertrude Tuckwell on the industrial : and, unique in her contribution, Beatrice Webb.

The leaders were always there. Behind them, however, whether on the political or industrial side, there were always tens, nay hundreds of women, quietly devoted, inspired by their devotion, who built up the solid foundations of organisation. Their names cannot be recorded here. There would be too many of them. Yet no picture of the effort which has slowly and steadily led to the emancipation of the working woman would be complete or true which forgot them. The leaders never forgot them.

II

Historical order has been neglected in telling the story of the match girls' strike. That story, however, serves to suggest the spirit which created women Trade Unionists, and also some of the tremendous practical difficulties with which those who sought to create them had to contend. It is time, however, to go back, and rapidly trace the steps that led to the foundation of the Women's Trade Union League, and to give some account of its pioneering work.

It should not, of course, be thought that the idea of Unions for women, or women in Unions, started with the Trade Union League. It is much older. There were " female lodges " in the famous Grand National Trade Union which brought half a million workers together in the Chartist days. Moreover, the Lancashire weavers, from the first, took women into their associations, and insisted that they were paid on the same piece-work price lists as men. In the seventies of the nineteenth century the spinners followed suit, although they expressly reserved certain lines of work exclusively for men. But, much later than the 'seventies, the average Trade Union member outside Lancashire, like the average man and woman of that day, shut eyes to the very large body of women who had got to work and did work for wages. They grumbled that women's low rates pulled men's rates down ; they could not, however, see that the only safety for themselves was to get the women inside the Unions. They still held to the fantastic notion that women could, somehow, be kept out of industry if they were kept out of Unions. Of course there were, and that from the start, honourable exceptions to this general view. In the first half of the nineteenth century, the London book-binders more than once took up the cause of the women workers in the trade. Thus, in 1849, the women struck against a redoubtable female employer—Miss Watkins. This fight is memorable because it threw up one of the earliest leaders among working women whose name survives—Mary Zugg. She was quite a young girl at the time of the folders' strike ; when she died, twelve years later, of consumption, the Secretary of the Book-binders paid tribute to her rare qualities of character and mind, saying that " she was not only a wise leader ; she was a beloved one ".

The founder of the Women's Trade Union League was, like Mary Zugg, apprenticed to the skilled craft of bookbinding. She was Emma Smith, better known by her married name of Emma Paterson. She was born in Westminster in 1848—year of revolutions in Europe. Her father was a schoolmaster. Her keen spirit was evidenced by her learning a skilled trade ; and by her becoming, when but eighteen, secretary to the local society for Women's Suffrage—a bold action at the time. She worked with Miss Emily Faithfull in her gallant efforts to form societies among women printers. She was also Honorary secretary to the local Working-men's Club and Institute. Thomas Paterson was its secretary ; and in 1873 Thomas Paterson and Emma Ann Smith were married. Soon after they visited the United States. In New York Mrs. Paterson made contacts with a Typographical Society entirely run by women, and also with a Women's Umbrella and Parasolmakers' Union. Stimulated by this, she came back to England, full of new zeal for helping working women to help themselves. Moreover, she saw, quite clearly, how it had got to be done. Women workers were shockingly underpaid, even when they did work that required a delicacy of touch that could only be achieved by long training. They were being exploited, and, through that very exploitation, compelled to be dangerous to their male colleagues. The only remedy, as Emma Paterson saw it, was for the women to combine, and, since the men would not admit them to their Unions, to form Unions of their own. She would really herself have always preferred to see separate Unions of women, since she was a feminist with the ideas of her period ; whether or no, she was passionately keen on combination ; and, since women had got to prove to men that they were unionisable, her line was the right one, at the time ; and her work was of enormous value.

Although a frail creature of delicate health, she had enormous and endless energy. By 1874 she had got together a group of men and women, mostly of the middle-class, who shared her ideas, and with their aid, formed a society called, at first, the Women's Protective and Provident League, and, very soon, the Women's Trade Union League—a name that accurately described its object. The Committee from the first included two Trade Unionists—the Secretary of the London Bookbinders, and of the London Trades Council ; and they gave a great deal of real and practical help. The first plan was to set up one Union, which all working women could join. In Bristol this was tried out, and had some success at first, although it was not lasting ; in London, it was unworkable. Undismayed, Mrs. Paterson set to work in her own former trade of bookbinding ; with the help of the friendly secretary of the Men's Union, a Society of women employed in bookbinding was brought into being, and gathered up three hundred members ; within a year Mrs. Paterson could hand over the Secretaryship to a girl herself working at the trade, Miss Whyte by name, who proved a tower of strength. This Society lasted till 1913.

The next groups to be worked were in what Americans aptly called the needle trades. The dressmakers were, at first, very keen : but they were not stayers. The upholstresses, however, were brought together : their society lasted ten years. Then it, too, winked out. In Yorkshire, Mrs. Ellis brought real qualities of leadership to an eight-weeks' strike of women weavers ; and thanks to her, they won. Soon afterwards, however, she shared the fate of many pioneers ; she was victimised by her employer and lost her job. Without her, the Union formed after the strike had no real hold. In Leicester another working woman, Mrs. Mason, stirred up her fellow-workers in hosiery. She was a woman of great ability ; she was elected to the local Trades Council—the first woman to achieve this honour ; and in 1877 she came as a delegate to the Trades Union Congress. This was the second occasion on which women had appeared there. Unhappily Mrs. Ellis died while still quite young ; without her, the Hosiery Women's Union languished.

From 1876 on, the Women's Trade Union League was invited to send delegates to Trades Union Congress. Whatever views the Trade Unions as a whole might take about women in industry, many Unions were most generous in their help, from this time on. Among the earliest who gave a helping hand were the Amalgamated Clothiers Operatives ; the London Compositors ; the Printers, Warehousemen and Cutters ; the Pottery Workers ; the London Cigar Makers ;

the Steel Smelters ; the Tin and Sheet Millmen ; the Chain Country Workers ; the Sheffield Hand File Cutters. All of these either admitted women to their own ranks or, more often, helped to form a women's section. Yet progress was certainly very slow.

Emma Paterson was, as were most advanced feminists in her day, opposed to protective legislation for women. Here not all her own colleagues agreed with her, and many Trade Unionists strongly disagreed. Her personality, however, and her work inspired real respect. Congress listened to her with full appreciation of her services. When she died in 1886, at the untimely age of 38, some 37,000 women were in Unions—most of them of course in the textiles. To find a successor to Mrs. Paterson would have been difficult, had not a very potent personality already begun to influence the policy of the League, and to carry it along lines, somewhat different from hers, which led to an ever closer alliance with the Unions. This was Emilia Dilke.

In background, and in much of her previous activity, Lady Dilke seemed far enough away from women like Miss Whyte, Mrs. Ellis, Mrs. Mason, or even Mrs. Paterson. Yet in her, working women found one of their ablest and staunchest champions ; under her the Women's Trade Union League took great strides forward. Daughter of an Indian Army officer and granddaughter of an American loyalist from the state of Georgia, Emilia Strong showed, as a child, a marked talent for drawing. John Ruskin was the biggest formative influence in her young development and undoubtedly helped her to see the close connexion between the practice of art and the way in which men live ; her social passion and her artistic faculty developed together. When a beautiful girl of 21, she married Mark Pattison, Rector of Lincoln College, Oxford ; his scholarship deepened her bent in that direction, and before she was middle-aged she had become a world-recognised authority on the history of art, especially on the art of France in the eighteenth century. Her writings brought her into contact with distinguished men and women in all parts and in all ranks ; but the very fullness of her life sharpened her sympathy with and interest in lives less rich than her own ; above all, in the lives of women who worked. Their lot never ceased to concern and move her. She saw that working women would go on being oppressed so long as other women cared nothing about their fate, and did nothing to help them ; so long as women were looked upon, by men and by themselves, as inferior beings. Even in enlightened Oxford " Women's Rights " were still a subject of mockery when she formed a Society for Women's Suffrage there. She understood both the idealism and the philosophy of Trades Unionism at a time when many who claimed to be both Liberal and enlightened misunderstood and villified both ; she was a member of the Council of the Women's Trade Union League from its foundation. After her marriage, in 1885, at the grim crisis in his career, with Sir Charles Dilke, she could and did throw her whole energy into this work. Marriage with Dilke gave new scope to an interest which had been active with her all her life, since he was as keen as she to help the workers' movement, and for long had been the potent friend of Trade Unions and more particularly of the Shop Assistants.

From 1886, when she succeeded Emma Paterson as President, Lady Dilke was tireless in its service. She brought to it something that was entirely her own. She had the same exact, detailed and grounded knowledge of the world of labour that she had of the world of art ; to each she brought a special gift of illumination. She was an admirable speaker ; she was beautiful, to the last ; she had great personal charm ; her mind was of a high order. More significant, however, than any of these great gifts, and realised by all who came in contact with her, was a burning sincerity grounded in an intense and passionate faith. For her, the League was on crusade. She could make others feel that too.

> The name of Trade Union, which was once a name of shame, is the name of soldiers of labour, who are fighting to preserve to the nation all that is noblest in human life. They are fighting to deliver the sacred city of the spirit from captivity to the heathenish conditions of modern industry.

When she used the word " heathenish ", she meant fully what she said ; when she used the word " crusade ", she meant it, fully, too. Instinctively without the sense of class, she had an outlook far more modern than Mrs. Paterson's ; and a point of view far more constructive. Under her guidance, the League worked hard for the extension of the Factory Acts ; it encouraged Unions to affiliate. Her hope, always, was to see women admitted as full members to the men's Unions ; meantime, however, any organisation they could achieve on their own was a step in the right direction.

By 1906, there were some 167,000 women in Unions —again mostly in the Textiles, which accounted for 143,000 of them. In thirty years' work, the numbers had almost quadrupled. But they were still wretchedly low. Moreover—and this was the serious aspect—organisation had hardly begun to touch the characteristically women's trades—sugar confectionery and food preserving, box-making, laundries, millinery, dressmaking, clothing, domestic, hotel and restaurant service, or clerical work. Here it was terribly difficult even to make a start, both owing to the conditions of the work itself and the low wages paid. Behind the factory workers in these trades were the home workers, who represented the most helpless group in the whole area of industrial life. The appallingly low earnings of these home workers dragged down the wages of all women workers. Often widows, or wives of men invalided, or for one reason or another under-paid, they were slaves of a need which deprived them of any power of resistance. They must take whatever pay was offered, or starve.

Over the entire field of women's employment, with the single exception of the Textiles, low wages made it wellnigh impossible for women workers to pay Union contributions, however low they were fixed ; it made it almost impossible to keep up Union membership. For a moment a bright spark of hope would leap up ; a successful strike, like that of the match girls, would seem to promise real improvement ; then, under the weight of the dreary struggle to keep body and soul together, members fell away, and the hope died. Little Unions, started under the impulse of some stirring speech or visit by the organiser of the League, would last for a few years then wink out. Moreover, women workers were scattered ; it was hard to get at them, harder still to keep them together. The keenest spirits among them were apt to marry just when they were beginning to be useful ; when they married, they were, in nine cases out of ten, lost to the Union. The married women workers—and there were plenty of them, both in the Textiles, in the clothing trades, and of course among the home workers—were so over-driven, between the claims of work and their home duties, that they could do no more. They went on working because the home was so poor that every extra penny counted, and had to be watched and toiled for.

The League members and organisers worked hard and faithfully. But progress was deplorably slow. Indeed in 1903, when Mona Wilson resigned the office of Secretary, Lady Dilke met the committee in a mood, very rare with her, almost of despair. Day-to-day work depended on the Secretary. The time had come when, if they were to go on with any hope, she had got to find for that job someone quite remark-able. She must be someone more than an organiser, though she must be that ; someone who could rouse women to fight for themselves ; someone who would never give up ; someone who could resist the feeling that the task was hopeless and they were trying to drive piles into a swamp.

Lady Dilke told the Committee that the one person she saw who could fill the bill was Margaret Bondfield, one of their number. But she was an active organiser for the Shop Assistants' Union ; the Union was in the middle of a great campaign, in which both Lady Dilke and Sir Charles were deeply concerned, for improving the shocking conditions in shops ; poor pay, reduced by heavy fines and deductions ; the living-in system ; a total lack of personal freedom ; enormously long hours of work. Margaret Bondfield was doing work that could not be left or interrupted. Her refusal, however, made Lady Dilke feel desperate.

Then one day Margaret Bondfield came to her and said that she had found just the right person; had even got her living with her, in her little flat. At a Shop Assistants' Conference two years earlier she had been immensely struck by the speech made by a young woman delegate from Ayr; next year, that same young woman was there as head of the Scottish delegation; and the acquaintance had ripened into friendship. Now, Mary Macarthur had suddenly left Scotland and come south. Here, so Margaret Bondfield asserted, was the ideal person for the League job; she had brains, she had enthusiasm, she had courage; she had, Margaret believed, a spark of genius. True, she was only 23, but she was of the stuff of which leaders are made. J. J. Mallon and Will Anderson, both staunch friends of the League, spoke in the same strain. J. J. Mallon had been particularly struck by Miss Macarthur's shrewd criticisms of the balance sheet in her speech at Conference; here was something more than a speaker.

Lady Dilke, and Gertrude Tuckwell, her right hand in all Trade Union work, agreed to see Margaret Bondfield's swan. They had doubts. Doubts, however, disappeared on contact with Mary Macarthur. Certainly this was somebody quite out of the common, this shy, pale-faced girl in the tartan dress; there was, when she lit up, a fire in her eye and a quality in her brain that were remarkable. Here was a crusader; Lady Dilke recognised her, as Margaret Bondfield had done. This girl might make difficulties; in fact she did; but she would assuredly also make things hum; in fact, she did.

Lady Dilke died a year later, to be succeeded by Gertrude Tuckwell. Before she died, she could feel that with Gertrude Tuckwell to steer it and Mary Macarthur to create the wind that could blow it along, the ship of the Women's Trade Union League was safe for constructive voyages.

Within that year, Mary Macarthur had shown that she was the sort of person who never waits for things to happen ; she went out and made them happen. The little offices in Club Union Buildings off the Grays Inn Road were dim and quiet when she started work in the summer of 1903 ; there was a book-lined committee-room, with the frail head of Emma Paterson on the wall ; there was a small room for the secretary, without a telephone or even a typewriter ; there was an even smaller room where Sophy Sanger presided over the Legal Advice Department. Quiet did not last long, after the new secretary had found her feet. Very practically she began by getting the accounts into order. She had kept her father's books in his big shop in Ayr ; she saw to it that the League balance was on the right side, for almost the first time in its history.

Then she took up the task of getting the League " on the map " as we should put it nowadays. She went out, and made meetings, at works gates, or wherever she could get at the workers. She got her meetings reported in the press, which she fed with paragraphs and stories. She lobbied at Westminster, where she soon learned her way about, helped by Sir Charles Dilke. News of bad conditions here, dismissal of workers there, sent her flying up and down the country ; and wherever she went she lit a spark of hope and communicated energy. Neither bad weather, long journeys, thin audiences, or even brickbats, ever kept her away, if there was a chance to deliver her message. There was something in that message that fired even the most hopeless with new courage. Magnetism she had in the highest degree; and an endless power of sheer hard work. Soon the little dingy office had become the focus of everything that affected the lives and conditions of working women. Mary Macarthur started a paper; she got a club going; above all she roused the public to knowledge and stirred it to sympathy.

There is something very exhilarating, even now, in the spirit of eager enterprise and unwavering faith with which the League office hummed in these days; and in the trio of women whose co-operation made it possible and kept it going. Mary Macarthur, Margaret Bondfield and Gertrude Tuckwell are not only women to whom all other women owe an infinite debt; in their combination they created a force no one of them could have contributed alone. The very differences in their personalities made this combination the more effective.

Margaret Bondfield represents in her own person the achievement of her sex in the period of her lifetime. The poor girl who went to work in a small local shop at 14 plus was, within a quarter of a century, to be the first woman elected to serve as chairman of a Trades Union Congress, and the first woman to hold ministerial office in a British Cabinet. From the West where she was born and raised, she came, at 18, to London, with only one or two references and a guidebook, to look for a job at a time when Employment Exchanges did not exist. The job she got gave her ten shillings to spend for a week of 76 hours; and compelled her to live in, under conditions that made the self-education she nevertheless accomplished, something little short of a miracle. She learned to write, through writing; she learned to speak at the Conferences of her Union, which she joined so soon as she knew it was there to join. Then, for ten strenuous years she was assistant secretary to her Union. At that time, it had under 2,000 members of either sex, out of some 250,000 shop assistants. Before she left her job, the number unionised had risen to 20,000. Next she became a propagandist for the Independent Labour Party and rose rapidly to be one of the leaders in its councils. Throughout this time she worked with and for the League in the closest friendship with Mary Macarthur. With grand generosity, she recognised the genius of the younger woman. For three years they lived together; association in work and intimate personal comradeship were part of the life of each, almost from the day they met.

Mary Macarthur, a few years younger, came out of a comfortable home background which grew too narrow, indeed stifling, for her ardent spirit. Her father, a prosperous Scottish shopkeeper, intended her to be a " lady ". She insisted on learning a job; insisted, too, on thinking with her own mind. That mind was at once realistic and enthusiastic; sentiment in it was perpetually crossed by a vigorous sense of humour. Personal charm here, rooted in something deeper than the good looks of her young days; the flower and expression of vivid personality. It was personality that made her, invariably, the centre of any group : in the words later used by Beatrice Webb " the axle round which the machine moved ". Dominating, even domineering she could not help being; that dominance was always harnessed to impersonal ends. But whereas goodness is the word one finally finds to express the special quality of Margaret Bondfield, force is that which remains when one tries to sum up the qualities of Mary Macarthur.

Beside these two, holding them together and yet never holding them back, stood Gertrude Tuckwell. Quite simply and sincerely, she regarded them as stars for which it was her privilege to provide the firmament. If ever she could be induced to think for a moment that she had a contribution of her own to make, she would have said that it was no more than to carry on the tradition of her aunt, Lady Dilke. That she did do, in every sense. She had the grace of mind and person, the distinction of character and intelligence, and the force of unfaltering conviction of Lady Dilke. But she did far more than that. She gave to the League so long as it lived, and carried on, after it was fused into the larger Trade Union movement, not only a rock-like steadiness, but an enthusiasm nothing could dim or tarnish, and a total selflessness that lifted every incident of its work to the high plane of social endeavour. In her own person, she was, for everyone who encountered her, a living argument for the reality of Socialism and the unreality of class distinction. No difficulty could daunt, no setback depress her ; hers was the faith that looks through mountains. The continuity of the effort to organise women, and men, had, in her, a guardian of incomparable force and faithfulness. Again and again, her example revived the spirit of the faltering, and sent them back to the fight. To her all who work owe a lasting debt.

CHAPTER V

THE FIGHT FOR TRADE BOARDS

Emma Paterson had dreamed of one big Union for all women. Before long, her young successor, Mary Macarthur, was at work on the same idea in somewhat different form.

The stiffest problem before the League was not to get a Union for a given group of women workers into being; the drive and dash of their secretary could be relied upon to do that. It was to keep it in being, in view of the poverty and isolation of the members. Thinking over this difficulty, Mary Macarthur came to the conclusion that, instead of forming a series of small, and therefore weak groups, they ought to try to bring all the women outside the big trades, like the textiles and the clothing and boot and shoe workers, into a single Union, with local branches. Then, finance would be easier; it would be easier to keep members together if they were joined up to a bigger unit than their own; the secretary of the common organisation could speak to any given employer with the weight of a national organisation behind her. The comprehensive whole would be a Federation, whose branches could, if they were strong enough, take responsibility and do real work; but the central officers would lay down common policies for all the members and speak for all of them. This new Federation would in no sense supersede the Trade Union League—how could it, if she, Mary Macarthur, remained secretary of both?

She communicated her enthusiasm to Gertrude Tuckwell ; swiftly the plan went through. By the end of 1906, the National Federation of Women Workers, organised on the model of a General Labour Union, was successfully established, with over 2,000 members and 17 branches in England and Scotland.

The Federation was planned as a fighting body ; Mary Macarthur used it as such to the full. Six months later she claimed, when speaking at a big strike meeting in Paisley, " the right to convey a message of comradeship and good cheer from the 80,000 women Trade Unionists whom I represent "—and these figures were probably justified or about to be justified. J. J. Mallon, who was in the inner counsels throughout, said later,

> With the Federation and the Women's Trade Union League, Mary Macarthur and Miss Tuckwell wrought miracles. With all their camp followers in attendance, they were no more than a stage army, but they said that they were the women workers of Great Britain, and they made so much noise that they came to be believed.

The strength of the Federation was not, in fact, ever in its numbers. It was a force because of its brilliant and audacious leadership, and because it stood for an idea that had got to be translated into fact as much for the sake of men workers as for that of women. It was the living symbol of the woman worker who, through it, demanded to be recognised as a worker. When in 1920, the Federation, as a separate women's organisation, ceased to be, and its members entered the National Union of General and Municipal Workers *en bloc*, the purpose which its founders had always had in mind was achieved. By then, the Unions that would not admit women had become a small minority. By then, the great majority of Unions were campaigning to get the women workers in their trades inside. More than that. They were committed to a policy of getting them in on equal terms ; they were coming to look on them simply as fellow-workers.

For this, the Women's Trade Union League and the Federation fought throughout. The beginning had got to be the organisation of women as women. The reason for this was not only that the men's Unions still dreamed of keeping low-wage competitors out of the labour market—although that was the case. Behind this hostile and timorous attitude on the part of the many male Trade Unions and Trade Unionists lay a series of sufficiently grim facts. Women, not by any wish of their own, actually were dangerous to Trade Union standards, because they were weak, helpless, isolated, untrained, unable to refuse any terms an employer offered. They had to live ; sheer need made them involuntary blacklegs. Unscrupulously, employers used them to cut rates.

In fact, the way to building a decent wage standard for women, and for men, was blocked by what Mrs. Webb later called " the morass of sweating ". Sweating—horrible name for a still more horrible thing—was the doom of hundreds of thousands of workers. It was the characteristic condition of great masses of women workers, outside the few organised industries.

About the turn of the nineteenth into the twentieth century there was a genuine, if not very effective, stirring of the public conscience about this. People woke up to the fact that the wealth and splendour of the Victorian era was under-propped by appalling poverty, and that this poverty was the lot of a great part of the citizens of the Empire. The work of the Salvation Army cast a searchlight on this " condition of England " as it was then called. In 1889, the publication of Charles Booth's great survey of conditions in London produced a shock ; in successive years came other inquiries which showed that London had no monopoly of destitution and degradation ; York, West Ham, Dundee, Sheffield revealed the same ugly pictures. Seebohm Rowntree's inquiry into conditions in York was particularly disquieting ; in a quiet Cathedral city, more than a third of the inhabitants were found to be below the poverty standard. York, in this, typified Britain. In 1890, a Committee of the House of Lords investigated sweating and defined it as " earnings barely sufficient to sustain existence ; hours of labour such as to make the lives of the workers periods of almost ceaseless toil, hard and unlovely to the last degree ; sanitary conditions injurious to the health of the persons employed and dangerous to the public ".

The people who endured these conditions were, in the main, home workers. Very often they worked for contractors and sub-contractors. They were apt to be isolated ; there was practically no possibility of organising them, so long as underpayment went on. If one worker refused a starvation price, there were dozens of hungry others to take her place.

The Report by the House of Lords Committee produced a stir. Nothing was done, however. People forgot things disagreeable to remember. In the House of Commons, Sir Charles Dilke raised the question again and again. He introduced a private member's Bill, to set up Wages Boards to fix minimum rates, as had been successfully done in Australia, since 1895. But he could not rouse either his fellow-members or the

Government. It was plain that there would be action only when there was a strong public demand for it. There was no such demand. The public went to sleep ; sweating went on.

It went on. At every turn, the Women's Trade Union League came up against it, and found any stable organisation of women workers rendered impossible, because of it. Gertrude Tuckwell and Mary Macarthur were convinced that Sir Charles Dilke's remedy, based on the experience of Australia, was the right one ; nothing could be done until Wages Boards were set up with the power to fix rates below which payment must not fall. But how were they to get the public roused ? How were the facts to be brought home to people's minds, so that they were felt ?

At last, a way to do this was found, by Mary Macarthur and J. J. Mallon, with the aid of A. G. Gardiner, then editor of the powerful *Daily News*. In Berlin, a great effect had been produced by the holding of an Exhibition of Sweated Industries ; why not hold one in London ? In 1906, it was held. Artificial flower-makers, hook and eye and button carders, sack-sewers, shirt-makers, fur sewers and pullers, tennis and racket ball-makers, box-makers, chain-workers, lace-workers and many others were assembled ; the starvation rates paid were set out, and the lamentable family budgets exhibited. Most effective was the sight of the wretched workers themselves, and the miserable stories they had to tell. An Anti-Sweating League was formed. Its first task was to convince the organised workers. A Conference was held in the Guildhall. Its verdict was more than uncertain until Mary Macarthur spoke ; after that, the Trade Union movement was committed to the principles of a minimum wage as the only effective remedy for sweating. Trade Union leaders like Arthur Henderson and D. J. Shackleton became enthusiastic advocates of Trade Boards.

The Election of December 1906 brought to the House of Commons a real Labour Party. One of its first acts was to press for and secure a Select Committee to inquire into sweating. Many members of this Committee were strongly opposed to any " interference " with wages ; but the evidence, and notably that of Mary Macarthur, converted them. She brought sweated workers to the committee ; she told how she had herself got diphtheria from handling baby garments made by a sick girl—paid at the rate of one penny per garment—so poor that at night she had to cover herself with them in lieu of the bedclothes she had not got ; she convinced the employers that the sweating contractor was their own worst enemy. Her most telling argument was that in favour of making the good employer's practice the standard for the trade ; on this a member of the Committee, by no means sympathetic at the start, told her that her evidence had brought Trade Boards within the sphere of practical politics. The Committe's Report recommended that Boards with power to fix rates to be enforced by Government inspectors should be set up. In 1909 Winston Churchill piloted a Bill to this effect through the House of Commons. Under it, Boards, representative of employers and workpeople, with an impartial chairman, were to be set up forthwith for four trades—chain-making ; machine lace-making ; paper box-making ; and tailoring (wholesale and bespoke).

In Cradley Heath in the Black Country, Mary Macarthur had already been at work, and there was the nucleus of a Union. It was possible therefore to get the two sides together ; to fix a rate took time and much patience ; but by May 1910 chain-making rates were fixed. For most of the women who made the roughest chains, often in their own backyards, the new rate was double or even treble what they had earned. Indeed, chain-making showed the difference between men's and women's conditions at their sharpest. Through the efforts of Tom Sitch, the men were well organised ; they worked reasonable hours for tolerable wages. The plight of the women was far different. A woman working in a little forge in her yard was lucky if she got 7*s*. or 8*s*. a week, out of which she had to find tools and fuel. The lowest rent for a two-room house and back-yard workshop was 3*s*. a week ; tools and fuel cost at least 2*s*. ; coal too had to be paid for. The women mostly worked for middlemen ; the men for large employers.

The new rate was fixed in May ; under the Act, however, six months had to pass before it became legal. In this six months the worst employers piled up stocks, so as to dispense with workers later ; they also persuaded many workers to sign forms contracting out of the new rates, by telling them that, at those rates, they would get no work. Some thirty firms, outside the Employers' Association, and some 140 middlemen, did this. There was one chance only of defeating this conspiracy against the Act ; to mobilise the good employers. This Mary Macarthur at once did ; they promised to pay the new rates. Thereupon, she called on all workers offered less than the new rates to come out on strike. The risk was tremendous, and she knew it. Heroically, the women rose to the challenge. They knew what it might cost them ; but Mary herself, and her aide, Julia Varley, had fired their hearts with hope and courage.

The struggle was severe. Mass meetings and processions kept up the spirits of the strikers in Cradley Heath. In London, funds were collected to help them. The Unions rallied to their cause, with organisers and cash. For ten weeks, the women stayed out. At last, a majority of the middlemen were ready to sign the White List. At a great rally, the women heard that the fight was won. They could hardly believe it. " It's too good to be true," they muttered, weeping with joy and relief ; hardly able to take in the change that was now coming in their miserable hard-driven lives. Mary told them, truly, that their pluck and faithfulness had won the new rates. Now, they must all join the Union, and keep safe what they had won.

Had this Cradley Heath fight been lost, the whole drive for Trade Boards could have failed ; the Act could have become a dead letter. It was won ; in Cradley Heath, the Trade Board was soon in full working order. Mary Macarthur and her helpers passed on to Nottingham, to cope with the terrible conditions in the machine lace trade. No organisation, here, of any sort ; it had to be created before the fight for a Board could begin, since the workers must have representatives before rates could be discussed. It was done ; a Board was set up and rates fixed. Tailoring and paper box-making Boards soon followed : again after hard work by the Federation.

Organised labour, both in the House of Commons, and in the Unions, gave a backbone to the movement for the legal regulation of wages in sweated trades, and pushed through the Trade Boards Act in 1910. On this stand, the Trade Unions have never gone back. Both at the time and since, however, there was a strong undercurrent of doubt and criticism ; nor has this ever disappeared entirely.

When the issue is looked at from the standpoint of theory, doubt and criticism are just enough. Trade Unionism aims at the building of such a strong and comprehensive organisation that free collective bargaining may everywhere fix decent rates and conditions for workers. From this standpoint, interference by the legislature to fix rates might well seem dangerous.

Those Trade Unions, however, which had striven to organise home workers, workers in scattered industries, workers employed by small men and by middlemen, found themselves compelled by hard and disagreeable facts to take a different view—a purely practical and realistic view. They found organisation everywhere hampered by the swamp of sweated labour. No solid ground, here, to build on : instead, a constant and most serious danger that gains won by long and strenuous Trade Union effort were going to be lost, and workers sucked down into a swamp, which threatened the organised trades on every side. Sweating was a threat to every established standard ; it encroached on every trade. Nothing in fact, as practical organisers knew, so urgently necessary, at once from the human and from the Trade Union standpoint as, somehow, to get piles driven into the swamp. Until that was done, no gains that had been won, no rates that had been fixed, could honestly be regarded as secure.

No theory could stand against the compelling argument of these facts. The sweated workers needed help, desperately. They were not only a misery to themselves. They were a danger to all workers. The case was clearest among women. But it was not a women's case only. There were male workers, in large numbers, whose lot was as deplorable. Mary Macarthur fought a battle for all workers when she convinced the House of Commons Committee and the Trade Unions; and when she fought successfully to get Trade Boards set up and minimum rates fixed.

The Unions were convinced. They accepted the view, from 1910 on, that to have rates fixed below which wages might not fall, made it easier, not more difficult, to get higher rates.

The essence of the Trade Boards method is the fixing of minimum rates by discussion between the two sides—employers and employed, with the guidance of an impartial chairman. The first great difficulty—met with in the setting up of the earliest Boards, and also with the much later ones—is to get representative bodies into being. This is a difficulty on the Employers' side, as well as on that of the workers; the worst employers strive to stay outside, as in Cradley Heath. Both on the early Boards, as on those set up later, the spokesman on the workers' side has often got to be a Trade Unionist who is not in fact a worker in the industry concerned, although tremendous efforts are always made to get a Union into being in trades where Boards function; and the existence of a Board is a factor that helps in that direction.

Throughout the whole struggle against sweating, invaluable service in the guiding of the workers in industries covered by Trade Boards has been rendered by the various General Labour Unions. Since the day of the earliest experiment, they have provided encouragement and also practical leadership. They have, in so doing, helped to foster Union membership.

It will be, at this point, convenient to sketch the development of Trade Boards, in very broad outline. So soon as the first four Boards had been got on to their feet, there was a great campaign for the extension of the method to other sweated workers ; in all this, the Women's Trade Union League was in the forefront of the fight ; and some of its most heroic episodes occur in connexion with these struggles. Thus, in 1911—which will always be remembered as a year of general and spontaneous industrial unrest—the great London Transport strike of the summer was in its last week when the sweated women workers of the Bermondsey factories—jam, confectionery, biscuits, pickles, canned food, glue, tin boxes, tea-packing, perambulator-making —suddenly came out *en masse* on strike. There were thousands of them ; they had no reserves, no organisation, and no savings. Mary Macarthur appealed to the public not for money but for food for starving women and children ; the public responded. By a miracle of devoted service, the vast supplies poured in were distributed to the strikers. The women were animated by an amazing enthusiasm and lightness of heart : yet the actual situation was an extremely complicated one. The women and girls worked for a great variety of employers, who were hardly better organised than they were ; there was indeed not one strike, but twenty separate strikes. Nevertheless, after three weeks, in which the gallantry of the strikers was extraordinary and extraordinarily sustained, wage advances were secured in all but four cases, the increases ranging from one to four shillings a week. After this, there was a rush to join Unions ; and finally, early in 1914, a Trade Board was set up for food preserving and sugar confectionery.

Other successes were the establishment of Boards for shirt-making and for workers in the steel-sheet and hollow-ware trades. More trades were scheduled; but the outbreak of war in the late summer of 1914 interrupted the plans laid. During the war no new Boards were set up. In 1917, however, the Women's Employment Committee of the Ministry of Reconstruction urged that, once the war was over, a slump was certain. To meet and mitigate its effects on the weakest groups of workers, there ought to be an extension of Trade Boards. In 1918, as a result of their pressure, a new Trade Boards Act was in fact placed upon the statute book.

The 1918 Act differed from the original Act in important respects. Under the 1910 Act, a Board could only be set up where wages were demonstrably too low. In 1918, however, they could be set up on this ground and also where, in the opinion of the Minister of Labour, there was " no adequate machinery for the efficient regulation of wages ". This was a big step forward. It registered the change in the public view of Trade Unions which had taken place; it also reflected the hopeful attitude towards social improvement which persisted for the first few years after the close of the war. Associated with the name of Mr. J. H. Whitley was a big movement for arbitration, conciliation, and industrial reconstruction, represented in the Industrial Councils since known by his name. The Committee over which he presided indeed looked forward to a time when every organised industry should have its Industrial Council, composed of representatives of Unions and employers; behind these were to be Trade Boards in all the unorganised Trades. The Act of 1918 did not go so far as this; but it did lead to

75

the setting up of a large number of fresh Boards. Aerated Waters ; Boot and Floor Polish ; Button-making ; Cotton Waste ; Dress-making ; Made-up Textiles ; Milk Distribution ; Perambulator- and Invalid Carriage-making ; Rope, Twine and Net ; Sack- and Bag-making ; and the Tin-Box Trade were among those covered by the new Act.

The slump of 1921 brought a heavy reaction in opinion, and a general attack by employers on Trade Union standards and wage rates. It also brought a strong campaign against the Trade Boards. All sorts of charges were suddenly levelled against them, and the Government was compelled to set up an Inquiry into their working, presided over by Lord Cave. The Report of his committee, issued in 1922, disposed of these charges, and stressed the usefulness of the Boards ; nevertheless, under the Conservative regime, no new Board was set up ; a change only came with the advent of Labour to office, when there was a considerable extension of the principle.

Before the Cave Committee, the Trades Union Congress General Council gave evidence strongly in favour of the Trade Boards ; a Special Advisory Committee of the Council was set up, to watch over and help them. Certain Unions, however, remained unhappy about the Boards, on the ground that where they existed there was no stimulus to joining a Union, while the minimum legally fixed tended to become the maximum. The very careful investigations conducted by the Advisory Committee, which took evidence from the Unions making complaints, found the weight of evidence in favour of the Boards, and this at a time when their operations covered something like a million and a quarter of workpeople, in a very wide range of occupations. The Boards are, in fact, doing work that could not otherwise be done ; they are protecting some of the weakest of workers.

It is not to-day open to doubt that through Trade Boards the conditions of some of the weakest and previously most oppressed workers in the community have been steadily improved. It is disappointing that the crutch provided by this piece of machinery should still be indispensable : that there are still many lines of work to which Trade Board conditions need to be extended ; and that the supervision they afford is still, in the industries they cover, incomplete. But the experiment has justified itself ; no-one to-day would ask for the abolition of the Boards.

The Act of 1910 was the successful outcome of one among the myriad campaigns on which Mary Macarthur and her comrades in the Federation and the Women's Trade Union League were constantly engaged. It was an important item in the social reform programme of the years immediately before the Great War of 1914—a programme that includes school feeding, school medical services, Old Age Pensions, and the establishment of National Health Insurance, and, on a very limited scale, at first, unemployment insurance. So far as women were concerned the original provisions of the Health Insurance Act were largely, as Mary Macarthur pungently put it, " a leap in the dark " ; the energies of the Federation were thrown vigorously into the fight for improvement and the provisions of the Amending Act of 1913, which made maternity benefit the property of the woman herself were largely the result of a campaign in which Margaret Bondfield was a leader. The Federation became the Approved Society under the Act for women workers ;

77

this involved an immense amount of work, and the offices had to be transferred from their original rooms in Club Union Buildings to Mecklenburgh Square—a house very near to that in which Mary Macarthur and her husband, Will Anderson, had the home which was at the same time a workshop.

Then, in 1914, were called, her and the Federation, to new, serious and unprecedented tasks.

CHAPTER VI

1914

To most citizens of Great Britain, war, in 1914, came as a sudden clap of thunder. There had been no long period of apprehension, anxiety, preparation, threats, violent attacks on peaceful neighbours. Germany was a country, like another ; the ordinary man and woman had no hostility to its form of government and nothing but friendliness for its people. With the great Social Democratic movement, there, the British Labour and Trade Union movement was linked by many ties of common work and aspiration.

In 1914, again, " foreign affairs " were, to the plain man and woman, still a dark mystery. Even the politically-minded hardly concerned themselves with them. Trade Unionists were aware of international affiliations, and of a strong sense of international solidarity ; but outside the organised movement, there was an astounding ignorance of and indifference to, these ties, and what they meant ; and a readiness, which now seems incomprehensible, to leave non-domestic issues to those professionally concerned with them. Only a handful even of Labour M.P.'s realised their relevance. There is a tremendous change, here. In 1914, the headlines " To Hell with Servia " expressed the typical British view of more countries than that unhappy little Balkan state.

One explanation of this aloofness is the fact that, at this time, home affairs were specially and even painfully absorbing. For the last three years, there had been a deep and growing unrest, industrial, political and social. In the House of Commons, feeling ran high on such great issues as Ireland : Women's Suffrage : Peers versus Parliament. The struggle over the Parliament Act had been the subject of two General Elections within as many years ; the conduct of the Diehards in the House of Lords had led to something like a constitutional revolution. On both sides, passionate class feeling was aroused. Preparation in Ulster for armed resistance to the Home Rule Bill, supported as it was by high officers in the Army and by the leaders of the Conservative Party—ready to accept foreign aid for the purpose of thwarting the expressed will of the majority —deepened this class antagonism. In Ireland, civil war was, in August 1914, on the point of breaking out.

Moreover, the same restless and excited temper was evidenced throughout the world of industry, which, from 1911 on, was in ferment. 1911 and 1912 saw major strikes in a series of great industries and the formation of the Triple Alliance of miners, railwaymen and transport workers. In 1913, there were no fewer than 1,497 separate disputes ; and in the first half of 1914, 937 strikes. Throughout these hectic years, strikes were largely unauthorised. Younger leaders toyed with syndicalism ; direct-action propaganda spread like wildfire through the rank and file. There was plenty of justification for all this ; although, thanks in part to the inflow of gold from South Africa, the country was rich, and the display of wealth crude in its extravagance, wages were low even in the best organised occupations, and prices rising. Discontent was not confined to " rebels ". Trade Union membership was mounting fast. Between 1910 and 1914, the increase in Trade Union membership was from 2,369,067 to 3,918,809. This increase was, in part, due to the National Insurance Acts ; it was, however, at the same time the register of a keen fighting spirit : a new and vigorous resistance to poverty in the midst of plenty. Unrest affected women workers as well as men. Some of the outstanding strikes were in the depressed and oppressed women's trades, like the great outbreak in Bermondsey in 1911, which Mary Macarthur carried to victory on the tide of public sympathy.

When war came in August 1914, the whole of this intense activity and this smouldering feeling was, over-night, transformed and transfused into patriotic enthusi-asm. There was a rush to the colours. Strikes were called off " for the duration ". The women's suffrage agitation was called off. Home Rule was put in cold storage. Accepting this, in a great patriotic gesture, John Redmond signed his death-warrant as a leader. Keir Hardie and Ramsay MacDonald seemed likewise to sign theirs, when they refused to share in the heady ardours of the hour, in which the great mass of their followers were deeply involved, and, protesting against the Declaration, went into opposition.

The various wings of the Labour movement, however, deep as their differences on the war—and throughout its course these differences persisted : there was none of the unanimity of 1940—at once closed ranks for the purpose of protecting workers from its immediate hardships. It was then axiomatic that war would bring severe and probably protracted unemployment. Within a few days of the Declaration, the War Emer-gency Workers' National Committee was formed, on a comprehensive basis, both political and industrial

leaders of all sections being drawn in. Mary Macarthur was from the first on the Executive.

Within a month, it was plain that unemployment
was to be even more severe among women than among
men ; over 19,000 women were in fact destitute.
Work-rooms were at once opened, and a variety of
temporary experiments tried ; it was at this period
that a contact was established between Queen Mary
and Mary Macarthur that lasted on, in strong mutual
respect and regard. At first the problem was grim ;
very soon, however, under the new pressure of war
demands for equipment, the tide began to turn. By
March 1915, the number of women unemployed had
fallen to 30,000 ; a serious shortage of male labour
was also beginning to make itself felt, partly, of course,
as a result of the system of voluntary enlistment. By
the hundreds of thousands, men poured out of vital
industries and services into the army. The new armies
—our own and those of our Allies—required munitions
on a vast scale, far beyond what had been anticipated
by those who dreamed in terms of a short war. The
concurrent supply of men and of munitions could not
be achieved unless women were, and in great numbers,
drafted into industry. At the same time, the help of
women was needed to carry on the normal work of the
country. Two huge demands were in fact made on
them at one and the same time—to carry on normal
work, and to make possible a vast production of an
immense number of things needed for the waging of
modern warfare.

The women were called. They came. They came,
in part, from occupations which had been put out of
business by war—from shops, from domestic and hotel
service, luxury goods manufacture, commercial occupa-

tions. They also came, and in very great numbers, from the ranks of women in all classes previously unoccupied, whether strictly, or only in the Census use of the term. They were thus new workers ; they were of all ages and of all types. A large proportion of them, of course, were married.

The change-over did not take place without muddle, friction, waste and hardship. The response of the women was magnificent. They were by no means always or generally magnificently treated. On the contrary, the view taken, and acted on, in many quarters was that, for them, patriotism was enough. They ought to be glad to work for long hours, under insanitary conditions, for wages that by no means kept pace with the fast rising cost of living. Ample forces were indeed massed to exploit their eager enthusiasm.

Now, however, the strenuous efforts to build up an organisation representing women workers bore fruit. There, ready for the fray, was the National Federation of Women Workers. In these fierce years of war, in fact, Mary Macarthur was in her element ; then, she did some of her finest and most lasting work. It was work that shortened her life. But it was work for which she would, had she been offered the choice, have gladly had her life shortened. She was the spear-head of a grand corps of workers. The stalwarts of the Federation and of the Women's Trade Union League threw all they had into the fight. As it went on, she gathered about her and trained new, young leaders : the leaders of the women's movement of to-day.

Her battle was for women, and for Trade Union standards ; she always saw the two aims as part and parcel of the same struggle. Very soon, too, she got the weight of the organised Labour movement swung

into the fight for decent treatment for the new women
workers.

The centre was of course the munition-making trades.
But what is true of the fight there is also true of clothing
and textiles, transport, boot and shoe, hosiery, chemicals, banks, the land, and the civil service. From 1916
to the end of the war, the employment of women
increased in all types of occupation, including many
previously barred against them. So, on the land, in
banks, in clerical employment of all kinds, in industry
and transport, women did work they had not been
allowed to do before. The number of women employed in Finance and Commerce increased from
506,000 to 955,000 ; in the professions (including
many ranges of clerical employment), from 51,000 to
120,000 ; in transport, from 18,000 to 115,000; in
the civil service, from 66,000 to 225,000 ; and in industry, from 2,179,000 to 2,975,000. Under industry,
the most striking increases are chemicals—40,000 to
103,000 ; and metals—170,000 to 596,000. This latter
figure includes Government establishments ; in them,
the increase was from 76,000 to 275,000.

Interest of course centred on the munitions industries.
Here, in engineering, was the most arresting case of the
new entry of women on a large scale to the kind of
employment they had not been permitted to do before.
The immense expansion of production here was accom-
panied, and made possible, by large-scale introduction
of new machinery, much of it automatic or semi-
automatic. This had begun before the war ; and had
led, already, to an increased employment both of
women and of semi-skilled and unskilled men and
juveniles in an industry once the strict preserve of the
skilled craftsman. Employers, now, eager to use the

new machine possibilities to the full, also desired to reduce their labour costs by increasing the proportion of unskilled as against skilled workers in their plants. They had a patriotic motive ; they also had an eye to profit, now and in the future. The Engineering Unions of course saw the danger plainly. Still craft Unions, in theory, they had fought against the introduction of the unskilled and semi-skilled man, if not very successfully. They now fought against the introduction of the even more dangerous unskilled woman. So, what was known as " dilution "—the watering of skilled workers by unskilled or semi-skilled—soon became, and stayed, the most hotly contested issue in the labour field. It was by no means an issue in engineering establishments only. It was an acute issue wherever new machinery was installed for war-time production purposes, and wherever new and previously inexperienced workers were taken in. This covered practically the entire field of war production and distribution. The drive for a sudden, large-scale increase in output in part created the problem. In part, however, the problem was always there, as an element in the incessant endeavour of the employer to reduce his costs, and especially his labour costs.

Now, the Trade Unions, while ready and eager to do all in their power to help to maximise output, were not prepared to allow a general alteration, on processes and on rates of payment, to be carried through, to their permanent disadvantage, by employers who used the cover of patriotic zeal to mask a long-range design. At the time, the stand taken by the Unions was, of course, largely misunderstood by the general public. The public, and the Government, thought only in terms of the war. Workers and their representatives had got to think also in terms of human life now and after the war. Keen as they were to make their contribution to victory, they had got to resist uncontrolled dilution and the unregulated variation of processes and rates. They had to get safeguards for the future, while they accepted substitution now.

The Engineering Unions did not then, any more than they do now, admit women to membership. This was a serious weakness in their armour ; a serious handicap to them in negotiation. It would have been much more serious, for them, as for the women who were being drafted in in great numbers, had not the Federation of Women Workers, with Mary Macarthur at its head, been there, ready and able to put and hold to the women's case for decent treatment. This was, at the same time, the engineer's case. Mary Macarthur was, throughout, at one and the same time, the champion of the new woman war worker and of the Trade Unionist, whether he was fighting at the front, or retained in industry at home. She saw her problem quite clearly. Two things she was determined to accomplish—first, she was going to win decent conditions for the woman war worker. Second, she was not going to allow employers to take advantage of the ignorance and intense patriotic enthusiasm of these new workers to undermine rates and conditions which had been won through long and hard years of Trade Union struggle, to the lasting detriment of the men when they came back, and of workers generally.

It was a task that taxed all her skill and energy, and all the skill and energy of Trade Union leaders and others—notably G. D. H. Cole, then acting as adviser to the A S E—who fought by her side. Throughout, she and the women for whom she spoke and acted, played the game by the enlisted worker; from the start, women accepted the view, so far as war industries were concerned, that they had come in, not to stay, but for the duration.

The first fight was to get recognition for the women and the fact that they had a point of view and a right to be consulted. Women were actually not represented when the Government called the first conference on dilution with the leading Unions, in March 1915. They were not parties to the Treasury Agreement of that year, which was, later, to be the basis of the Munitions Acts. Of the Treasury Agreement, the first part made strikes and lock-outs illegal for the duration, and set up compulsory arbitration. In return for this substantial concession by the Unions, the Government pledged itself to restore previous Trade Union conditions and practices, in every case, after the war. On their side, the Unions undertook to relax existing demarcation restrictions, and to allow the employment of unskilled men and of women " provided this shall not affect adversely the rate customarily paid for the job ". This looked all right, but what exactly did it mean? What was " the job "? The large-scale introduction of new machinery was creating entirely new jobs—or what could be claimed to be new jobs. What, moreover, was " the rate "? Was it the piece-rate? Yes, said Mr. Lloyd George. Not, however, it appeared, the time-rate. That being so, employers were left, to all intents and purposes, free to fix women's time-rates as pleased themselves. As Mrs. Drake puts it in her invaluable book on *Women in Trade Unions* (to which every reader must go for a full account of the events sketched in this chapter) : " In munitions factories, not only were many thousands of women munition workers necessarily employed on time work, but in the general readjustment of processes, men's piece-rates had practically disappeared." She quotes a works manager as saying : " What on earth can one do when a girl is earning as much as 15*s*. a week but lower the piece-rate ? " Employers who hesitated in doing this had no compunction in cutting the time-rate. This was constantly done, especially under the premium bonus system. It would have been done to an even greater extent had not Mary Macarthur, with the Federation behind her, come forward to defend the women munition workers. She never let go, so long as the war lasted.

The first big case was that of the fuse and cartridge branch. There, the girls' conditions were notoriously bad. At a conference of Trade Unions and women's societies, held in London in the spring of 1915, women were urged to join the Unions, and the slogan of " equal pay for equal work " was adopted. In fact, women poured into the Federation. In June, a formal alliance was entered into with the Amalgamated Society of Engineers, and a claim was put forward jointly for a pound a week minimum for all substituted women in the engineering trades.

Although this was formally accepted, conditions in the shops remained bad. Wages far below a pound a week went on being paid, for long hours of very heavy work. By September 1915, discontent had become so serious and so vocal that the recently established Ministry of Munitions was compelled to set up a Labour Supply Committee, with Mary Macarthur as a member. The famous Circular L 2, put out by this Committee, definitely fixed a pound as the standard wage for a normal week, for substituted women over 18 years of age ; over and above this, they were to get overtime, Sunday, holiday, and night-work allowances, at the men's rates. Women replacing skilled men were to get the men's time-rates ; for others, premium bonus or piece-work rates were to be fixed, on the basis of the men's time-rates.

In Government establishments, Circular L 2 was honoured, and did improve conditions ; non-Government firms, however, carried on as before. They took advantage of the famous Leaving Certificate clause in the Munitions Acts to prevent workers from leaving, however intolerable their conditions. For the rest, in effect, they snapped their fingers at the provisions of the Circular. In these circumstances, the Government was forced, largely by Trade Union pressure, to bring in a fresh Munitions Act. This contained a clause giving the Minister power to fix wages, etc., for women *in all establishments* as from January 1st, 1916. From this time on, the £1 minimum became operative, although it took much time and continual struggle before it was enforced universally. Thus, early in 1917, Mary Macarthur wrote to *The Times* to point out : " There are to-day women working on munitions of war for 2¾d. and 3d. an hour." Applications for recourse to arbitration, as provided by the Act, took months to get through ; awards, when granted (and the Federation practically never failed to get an award), dated only from the date of issue of the award. Further, in too many cases the minimum remained the maximum. Rates for women who took the place of men continued to be lower than the men's rates had been ; often very much lower. The defence put up by the employers was that, otherwise, women would be earning too much. This was no doubt a tribute to their efficiency and hard work ; but the result was grave injustice.

In cost of living bonus rates, again, there were gross inequalities between rates paid to women and to men. Where a man got 16s. 6d. a week, plus 12½ per cent. on earnings, a woman got 11s. 3d., with no plus, although it could hardly be maintained that the rise in the cost of living did not affect either sex alike.

Low wages were not the only grievance from which women war workers suffered. Working places and conditions were, in very many cases, deplorable. Workers were over-driven ; hours were, at first, fearfully long. For 12 or even 14 hours, day or night, and for seven days a week, they toiled in works where sanitary arrangements were totally inadequate, and safety precautions conspicuous by their absence. The Factory code was of course in abeyance. It took continuous pressure, in and out of Parliament, before employers learned that excessive hours were uneconomic, and that the health of workers was an asset in their output. Here, the main lever of improvement was of course Trade Union action ; until the women were got into the Unions, there was little prospect of effective relief for them. Those Unions which had rules against the admission of women now for the most part relaxed them, in order to take in the new war workers. Some, for instance the Transport Unions, absolutely forced them in, with excellent results, so far as their rates of pay and general conditions were concerned. Thus, on the railroads, substituted women got the men's minimum time-rates. Even here, however, there was a big difference in the bonus rate ; while a man got 35s., a woman got 20s. 6d. Motor drivers remained unorganised ; tram and bus conductors, however, were taken inside, and got the men's rates. In London, where the employers refused to give the women the men's advances, the women came out on strike, in defiance of Acts, and, supported by the men and by public opinion, won their case. It was this victory that led to the setting up of the War Cabinet Committee on women in industry, to which Mrs. Sidney Webb made a Report of which there will be more to be said, later.

Where women did get decent conditions, it was because they were organised. The National Union of Shop Assistants got something like four-fifths of the men's rate for its women ; opinion in the Union was against their getting more, despite the fervent appeals from inside, of Bessie Ward and other Trade Union leaders. Black-coat workers, on the other hand, suffered from the fact that they were not organised. The Government, a very large employer of clerical labour, was quite openly opposed to equal pay for women and men.

Most of the Unions made a big and a successful drive to get the women in. The ranks of the Engineering Unions, however, remained closed ; it was therefore into the Federation and into the Unions catering for general labour that the substituted women in munitions industries came in the main. Between the Federation and the Unions co-operating with it, a Joint Committee on Women's Wages was set up, and made full and effective use of the arbitration machinery. The Federation had a highly efficient band of officers. Its leaders, Margaret Bondfield, Susan Lawrence, Gertrude Tuckwell, were, like Marion Phillips, active in every phase of the fight. The Federation won over 90 per cent. of its arbitration cases. In the

other Unions, although women poured into membership in such numbers that in some cases they outnumbered the men, they had little say in policy or
management. Thus, out of the twenty-eight women
who appeared in 1918 as delegates to the Trades Union
Congress, no fewer than eight were members of the
Federation. It was the Federation which induced first
Trades Union Congress and, later, the International
Labour Office, to adopt its formula for equal pay for
the same job ; the Federation, too, supplied the drive
which led to the setting up of the Joint Standing
Committee of Women's Industrial Organisations, which
has ever since proved a most useful piece of Labour
machinery.

Valuable, in all this, as was the contribution of her
colleagues, there is no one of them, or of the eminent
persons whom she encountered in these years of strenuous and unrelaxing fighting, who would not hail Mary
Macarthur as the true lion of the battle for women of
the years from 1914 on.

It was a great battle. It was, too, a partially successful one. During the latter war years, large numbers of
women were making better earnings than they had ever
done before. A real advance of something like 50 per
cent. was won for women working in controlled establishments ; as also for women working in brass found-
ing, electrical trades, lamp, asbestos, cable, nut, nail
and bolts, optical instruments, small tools, explosives,
rubber, general aircraft, and aircraft wood-working.
Outside munitions, however, the advance secured
seldom did more than keep pace with the rise in the
cost of living ; and not always that. And even in
munitions, and to the end, women's cost-of-living bonus
remained lower than men's—11s. for a woman against

16s. 6d. plus 12½ per cent. on earnings, for a man. G. D. H. Cole sums up, in his *Trade Unionism and Munitions*, as follows : " Women were as a rule paid considerably less than men during the war, even on identical jobs, and were often paid less for identical amounts of work on systems of " payment by results ". But women's wages were only raised to the standards actually reached by persistent Trade Union effort and in the face of a chorus of complaints that they were being paid " more than they were worth ".

In fact, public admiration for women shell and fuse makers, although freely and even lyrically expressed, did not naturally or spontaneously translate itself into a desire, still less into a determination, to see that they were paid decently. Unremitting Trade Union pressure was necessary to extract from recalcitrant employers and a reluctant government decent working conditions and a living wage. It was not until a late stage in the war that they were secured. Relatively, women did earn more than they had done before ; absolutely, however, their new earnings did not in the average case do much more than keep up with the rise in the cost of living. The picture, figuring so large in the middle-class mind, of the fur-coated munition worker with her piano, was not often realised in fact ; when it was, very hard work had gone to its earning.

But for Mary Macarthur, women would have fared very much worse than they did. So would men. She fought, throughout, both for the women and the men. Her service, through the years of war, as through her whole career, was as great to Trade Unionism as to the women whose special champion she was ; she knew that it was, all the time, the same service. She never forgot, and she never allowed those who worked by her side to forget, that there was to be a world after the war.   She was out to prevent the exploitation of women in the present.   That took a great deal of doing.   She did it.   She insisted on having women treated fairly, for their own sake ; she also refused to have them used to pull down normal rates and worsen normal working conditions.   Men were coming back to their jobs after the war ; it was in their interest and in that of women that rates, whoever earned them, should be fixed at a living and not at a sweated level.   She knew that employers, in the constant effort to cut costs, found the presumed inferiority of women useful : useful, above all, for breaking rates.   War gave an unequalled opportunity for splitting up and " de-skilling " jobs ; to facilitate this process, and lastingly, they used, for all that it was worth, the argument that women, because they are women, cannot match a man's rate.   Once the process had been broken up, the rate paid at each stage in the new series was less, and often much less, than that paid to the man on the single process.   It was, moreover, then claimed that there really never had been anything in the original single process to justify a high rate on grounds of skill.

Nothing new in this.   Normally, of course, it is a constant element in mass-production techniques so to sub-divide operations as to lower basic rates, and substitute, first at this stage and then at that, unskilled and semi-skilled labour for skilled.   War conditions of course gave an extended opportunity for doing this, and even for doing it amid public applause.   Certainly, between 1914 and 1918, to a much greater extent than to-day, the claims of the worker to decent conditions and a right to live and not merely exist, were apt to be overlooked ; any reminder of them was apt to be dubbed "unpatriotic" by a large number of fairly comfortable persons. This, then, applied specially to any claims on behalf of women. The classic statement of the employer's standpoint, here, is quoted by Mrs. Drake from *The Engineer*, organ of the Employers' Federation, for October 1915:

> The fact of the matter is really not that the women are paid too little—or much too little—but that the men are paid too much for work that can be done without any previous training. High wages are paid on the false assumption, now almost obscured by Trade Union regulations, that it takes long to learn the craft. Everyone knows now, and all managers knew long ago, that no long period of training is necessary, and the whole argument of high wages based on long training falls to the ground.

Here, quite plainly stated, was the prospect towards which employers were working. It was perfectly plain to Mary Macarthur, as to the Trade Union leaders with whom she worked in close and loyal co-operation through four years of war. It was a prospect whose realisation she was determined to prevent; and did prevent. She knew that in preventing it she was fighting, at one and the same time, the battle of Trade Unionism and of women. Then, as now, it is, fundamentally, the same battle.

Therefore, since she knew well what she was about, it did not perturb her to be told that the fixing of rates at the Trade Union standard in this process or in that would mean, in the end, that a man would hold down the job. Merely to have large numbers of women employed, regardless of the conditions of their employment, was never an object with her. From first to last she fought, side by side with the Unions, whether or no they admitted women to membership, for the restoration of Trade Union conditions and practices. From that she never swerved. In March 1915 a pledge was given to this effect. At last, in July 1918, it was implemented in the passage through Parliament of the Restoration of Pre-War Practices Act. Throughout the intervening period, the Federation of Women Workers worked, whole-heartedly, to get this done. Mary Macarthur knew, they all knew, that one effect would be to hasten the withdrawal of women from war-time jobs. They knew, too, however, that the alternative was mass-unemployment for men, and an all-round lowering of the standard of living. Their choice was unhesitating and clear. In making it, they served men and women wage-earners, then and since.

CHAPTER VII

POST-WAR

WHEN the Armistice came, suddenly, on November 11th, 1918, women workers were dismissed by the thousand, in many cases between one day and the next. Most of them took their dismissal without protest. Relief and thankfulness for peace, after the long strain, were so intense that the hardships which peace actually brought to many were accepted and endured with striking fortitude. Here and there there were revolts. Twenty thousand women, abruptly paid off at Woolwich Arsenal, marched to Whitehall and succeeded in thoroughly frightening Mr. Lloyd George. The establishment of the out-of-work donation (later known as the dole) was in no small degree the outcome of their action. There were plenty of other hard cases. But the impulse that animated the generality of women war-workers was not revolt. The war was over ; thank God for that. They had done their bit. Some —perhaps the larger number—were glad to get back to their homes and their home tasks. Certainly for the vast majority the overwhelming thought was that, now, they would see their men again. Loyalty to those men indubitably came first. Even those who had most enjoyed their new personal freedom and the new experience of having money of their own earning to spend, cheerfully went back. For the duration they had worked hard and well. But they had been filling places which of right belonged to the returning soldiers.

E

The vastly increased wartime employment of women in industry, above all in the engineering and clothing industries, led to a very rapid increase in the number of women in Trade Unions. Most of the new women went into the National Federation of Women Workers or the general labour Unions. The Engineers still closed their doors. But in this they were practically alone. The broad effect of war conditions was to cause Unions to open their doors and keep them open. This meant a big stage had been completed in the work the Women's Trade Union League and the National Federation of Women Workers had been formed to do. Mary Macarthur, Gertrude Tuckwell, Margaret Bond-field and their fellow-workers had never wanted to keep women separately organised. Separate organisation had been a necessary, preliminary stage only. So long as many Unions would not admit women, women had to form Unions of their own. So soon as the men's Unions did admit women, even welcomed them, the work of the separate women's Unions was done.

By 1921, therefore, the National Federation of Women Workers, with its 80,000 odd members, had become a " district " of the General and Municipal Workers' Union—itself a fusion of a number of separate Unions. At the same time, the Women's Trade Union League was honourably wound up. The Trades Union Congress reserved two places for women on its General Council. The Standing Joint Committee of Industrial Women's Organisations was set up to provide machinery for bringing forward issues of special importance to women. There are still one or two smaller women's Unions, but the general tendency is definitely against sex demarcation. This is to-day the general outlook of men, as of women.

Post-War

The immediate post-war years were years of hope and great activity in the Trade Union world ; years of rising membership, and of large-scale amalgamations and consolidations between existing Unions, as well as the formation of new Unions, notably among non-manual workers. The new Unions formed by railway clerks, bank and insurance clerks, civil servants, draughtsmen, actors, musicians, doctors, local government employees, commercial travellers, teachers, and technicians of various kinds, from the first admitted women on equal terms. There arose a new sense of solidarity among workers, which affected the professionals as well as the manuals ; a positive realisation of identical aims and interests. This was reflected in the new constitution of the Labour Party, which stated firmly the common purpose and common loyalties of " workers by hand and brain ". At the time of the National Industrial Conference in 1919, indeed, it looked as though the common efforts and sacrifices of the war were going to bear fruit in a real charter for labour, accepted by employers, based on a minimum wage and a national limitation of hours of work.

These hopes were doomed to disappointment. The Coalition Government's handling of the post-war situation produced tragedy both in the international and in the domestic field. The pledges and promises of industrial reconstruction were not fulfilled. They proved to be part of the false post-war high-prices boom, which collapsed at the end of 1920 and was followed by the long post-war depression. This depression was, in its turn, accentuated by the Government's policy : the hasty de-control of industry, and above all, by the betrayal of the Miners. The Miners' defeat in 1921 was the signal for an attack all along the line by employers, who found deadly allies in the slump in the exporting trades and the rapid rise of unemployment. In 1920 the Agricultural Wages Boards were swept away ; soon, an attack on Trade Boards followed. In 1922 the Engineering employers locked out the members of the Amalgamated Engineering Union and of forty-seven other Unions ; after a dispute which lasted for four months, the men were beaten to surrender. The success of the Engineering employers encouraged further attacks. The Miners were once again in the forefront of the battle. Faced with fresh wage reductions, in 1925, they appealed to the Trade Union movement as a whole. The threat of action by the Triple Alliance frightened the Baldwin Government into setting up a new Commission and paying out a subsidy while it deliberated ; but when the Samuel Commission reported, the Government took no active steps to implement its findings. The owners stood pat on wage reductions ; the T U C promised full support to the Miners. They were locked out : the so-called " General Strike " of 1926 was not, in fact, general, since only the first line of workers were actually called out ; but they did come out, with total selflessness, in support of the Miners. Here was an attempt by stopping certain vital industries and services—mainly transport, railways, printing, electrical—to compel the Government to do justice to the Miners. Sir John Simon denounced it as " unconstitutional ", an endeavour to coerce the State ; but high legal opinion held that, since nothing was said in the Trade Disputes Act of 1906 to differentiate between political and industrial strikes, this strike was lawful. The Government, after breaking the strike and forcing the Miners to surrender, passed the Trade Disputes Act of 1927.

This of course expresses the Simon view. Under this Act, a strike is illegal *if* it has any object other than or in addition to the furtherance of a trade dispute in the industry in which the workers are engaged *and* is designed or calculated to coerce the Government either directly or by inflicting hardship on the community. This governing " if " and " and " is a matter which will have to be decided by High Court Judges. Since 1927 there has in fact been no major strike to provide grounds for such a judgment.

In addition to this general ruling, the 1927 Act excluded civil servants from affiliation to the Trade Union Congress or any other Federation of Trade Unions which takes in other than civil service members.

Perhaps the worst feature of the 1927 Act is its obscurity. It was designed, politically, as a blow at the workers, in their industrial and their political capacity ; it therefore reversed the 1913 Act, by providing that members can only be required to pay towards any political activity on the part of the Union—the running of candidates, or the promotion of parliamentary measures—if they expressly contract-in to the political levy. This provision has imposed very heavy work on Unions : in some the percentage contracted-in is high, in others low. An effective blow was certainly dealt by the measure at the finance of the Labour Party : and this was a main part of the intention of the framers of the Act.

In the events above summarily portrayed, women played no outstanding part. The storm centre was the mining industry ; there, women were deeply involved as mothers, wives, sisters ; on them a heavy burden fell ; their courage and endurance were constantly behind their men : but they did not, of course, directly figure as workers in the mining industry. Indeed it might appear, so far as women were concerned, that the pattern of the post-war years was simply the old pre-war pattern repeating itself : as though 1914–18, with their stress and stir, had simply faded out, like some theatrical transformation scene.

Industry returned, in the main, to its old ways. The wartime controls were hustled out of the way. The new mass-production methods were used as means for reducing wages and de-skilling jobs. Increased production, while possible, could only " pay " in the Capitalist sense if distribution were revolutionised. That problem nobody was ready to tackle. Employers, thinking on the old lines, reduced their home market by the attack on wage standards. War experience had not taught most of them to think of women except in terms of cheap labour ; and they were not sure how cheap women were. Summarising the Munitions experience in 1923, G. D. H. Cole wrote :

> The huge experiment of wartime production has not furnished any convincing data either for or against the value of women's labour. It has shown, indeed, that for its proper utilisation certain increased charges for supervision and adaptation of factory plant and methods must be incurred ; but of these supervision only need be a standing charge, and it is " non proven " how far this can be compensated for by higher output or greater docility.

During the war indeed, women's labour " failed to get quite a fair chance . . . to the end, women had to contend with the feeling, largely shared by the employer and the male workers, that they had no business to be in factories at all ". That feeling reasserted itself after the war. It grew stronger with the slump. Such jobs as there were, had got to be jobs for men.

It might appear, from all this, as though there were indeed no change. Yet there was a change : it was important and lasting, although it was rather psychological than immediately practical. After 1914-18, things were not again as they had been before. True, women were rushed out of industry almost as swiftly as they had been rushed in, and with no more consideration for their views about the matter. The men came back to their old places ; the women returned to their homes, or to women's work. After a year it seemed, to the superficial observer, as though nothing had happened. Yet two things of high significance had happened.

First, the Trade Union movement had been greatly strengthened, and neither the loss of membership in the post-war slump, nor the assault of the 1927 Act undid the lift in status and in general public esteem that it achieved. As it was put by Sidney and Beatrice Webb in the 1920 edition of their great *History of Trade Unionism* :

> The Government found itself compelled, in order to secure the co-operation of the Trade Unions, both during the war and amid the menacing economic conditions of the first half of 1919, to accord to them, and their leaders, a *locus standi* in the determination of essentially national issues that was undreamt-of in previous times. The Trade Unions, in fact, through shouldering their responsibility in the national cause, gained enormously in social and political status.

Neither the attack on wage-standards of the years from 1921 on, nor the 1927 Trade Disputes Act, could retard the steady growth of the movement, or its advance in general public respect and in self-respect. From the outset of the present war, public opinion was ready for the inclusion of Trade Union representation in the Government ; when the war situation became serious, public opinion demanded it. So soon as a truly national administration was set up, in May, 1940, Trade Unionists took leading places within it. Here is one of the major post-1918 social changes.

The other equally significant change is the change in the position of women. Not, as yet, in their economic position ; but, very definitely, in their social and political position ; in their status. By 1918, it was plain that public opinion about women's place in the world had changed. More important still, woman's own opinion about her place in the world had changed.

The clock could not be set back. Indeed, however slowly and irregularly, its hands have been moving forward, ever since.

The wartime discovery that women were of use to the community, nay, that, in time of stress, they were indispensable, achieved something that years of agitation had failed to accomplish. It made them citizens. For the best part of four years the nation had relied, and knew it had relied, on women to do some of its most necessary and important work. No pretending, after that, that women workers were not people ; and people entitled, in barest justice, to be regarded as full members of the state for which they had toiled. One by one, the crusted old opponents of women's suffrage were compelled to recant, more or less swiftly and more or less gracefully. Mrs. Webb and Mrs. Humphrey Ward came over ; so did, later, Mr. Asquith. True, in 1917, there were still people in high places, people even in the War Cabinet, who resisted. Thus Lord

Curzon fought in the last ditch ; it took the firm will of a Trade Unionist, Arthur Henderson, to overbear him. Henderson insisted that the Reform Bill must sweep away both property and sex qualifications against the exercise of the democratic right of franchise ; he asked the Noble Lord if he desired to see a revolution ? Curzon gave way. The Bill of 1918 swept aside sex disability as such, and gave women votes at the age of 30 ; ten years later, this insulting age discrimination was removed in its turn. In the 1929 Election, women voted on the same terms as men. To-day they are in a majority in the electorate ; yet no one has been able to show that there is such a thing as the " women's vote ", hard as some have tried. In 1918, there was a handful of women candidates, Mary Macarthur being among them ; but none, in Great Britain, got in ; while the Countess Marckievicz, returned in Ireland, refused to take her seat at Westminster. In 1929, fifteen women took their seats as members of Parliament, and one of them, Margaret Bondfield, was made a Cabinet Minister and sworn of His Majesty's Privy Council ; while another, Susan Lawrence, a past colleague in many fights for Trade Unionism for women, became a Junior Minister. Politically, women now enjoy an equality that is genuine and complete. As members of Parliament and of local governing bodies, they are treated, and look upon themselves, simply as members. The parliamentary salary takes no account of sex. There have been many woman mayors ; in its Jubilee Year, the London County Council chose Mrs. Eveline Lowe to preside over its deliberations and guide its policies.

Here lies the substance of a peaceful revolution ; and the lever that set it in motion was the woman worker.

She freed her sex, although she has not yet received the wages of her own freedom. Political emancipation has by no means, as yet, carried economic emancipation with it. But what is not yet achieved should not blind any to what has been won. The process of mental and moral release from long servitude is working itself out. Here the experiences of 1914–18 were a powerful and lasting stimulus.

It is true, of course, that the process was slow, and that it met with many a setback. In the minds of employers, and even of many male workers, the old outlook and the old prejudices die hard ; they are by no means everywhere dead. In the decade after the war, working conditions went back, in the main, to their pre-war shape. Of the women taken on during the war, something like a million soon returned, more or less contentedly, to the life they had lived before. They went back to their homes and their unpaid household drudgery there. Some endured severe and protracted unemployment, on a " dole ", of course, lower than the masculine. Those who remained in work suffered, with their male companions, and on their own lower rates, the slow hardships and steady wage-cutting of the long slump. It all looked much as it had done before. Women, as before, were getting the thin end of the stick.

Yet there was a difference. The emancipation of women was one of the forces that brought the condition of the ordinary home to the forefront in post-war legislation and administration, and kept it there. Here the co-operation between women and working men strengthened both. The Labour Party had been the first to put the political emancipation of women in its programme. It had been unfaltering in that allegiance, and, even in the economic field, carried a majority of Trade Unionists with it. After 1918, opposition was confined to a small minority : the movement as a whole was converted. The sense of justice and fair play, of the logic inherent in Trade Unionism, helped to bring about a change which, in its turn, has worked powerfully to make conditions for the women war worker of 1939 less severe than were those of 1914–18.

This change is very hard to measure ; but no one will deny that it is there. Even women who did not expect life to be different for themselves had, after 1918, new expectations for their daughters. Moreover their own outlook was more subtly and deeply altered than they always knew. One sign of this is the change in their outward appearance. This applies to the not-so-young as well as to the young ; it applies, very markedly, to the children. Those children are now, as can be observed in any elementary school, neatly and sensibly clothed and shod ; their hair is well-cut and cared for, however poor their parents. Much, here, is due to the school clinic, with its stress on health and hygiene ; and to the ante-natal clinic and health centre, with their instructions about sensible clothing and feeding. But there is a new attitude ; a new self-respect. In Lancashire, for example, the mill worker, before the war, was apt to be a shapeless bundle in shawl, with clogs on her feet. Now, she goes to work in neat if not always very practical shoes, in a short, well-cut, simple dress, with a hat placed at a stylish angle on her smartly curled head. Class distinctions have begun to vanish, so far as the clothes of the younger women are concerned. More than this : women have begun to look after their health as well as their appearance ; and look younger, at 40, than their predecessors did at 30. These are small things. Yet they are the outward marks of deep and far-reaching inward change. Young women take to-day a less humble and more hopeful view of themselves and of their work than many of their elders did. There is a new self-respect, which affords the right basis for Trade Union organisation, and promises its steady extension.

CHAPTER VIII

A BRIEF SURVEY OF CERTAIN MAJOR EMPLOYMENTS

In the original plan of this book, a main place was to have been filled by a detailed survey of conditions in every important trade and branch of work occupying women.

Circumstances have prevented this ; and the pages that follow are admittedly incomplete. They cover only certain main trades in which active Unions exist.

I. THE TEXTILE GROUP IN GENERAL

In any survey of women at work, the Textile trades must come first. The processes of spinning, weaving, finishing, bleaching and dyeing cotton, wool, flax, hemp, jute and silk, whether natural or artificial, are among the oldest female employments. Eve traditionally spun, while Adam delved. The Hosiery and Clothing trades are closely allied to the Textiles and present many of the same features. At the weaving loom and in the card-room, and as knitters and garment-makers, women outnumber men.

The Textile trades occupy by far the largest body of industrial working women ; they also represent by far the biggest Unionised group. In 1937, according to Ministry of Labour statistics, out of 1,170,000 employed in this group (excluding clothing), 720,000 were women. Out of a total of 450,000 cotton workers, 300,000 were women ; out of a total of 223,000 in wool and worsted,

130,000 were women ; out of 133,000 in hosiery, 108,000 were women ; out of 45,000 in jute and flax, 30,000 were women.

Textiles are not less important from the Trade Union standpoint. In both Cotton and Wool, organisation has a long and honourable history. In Cotton, collective bargaining was established long before it was won in other industries. In Cotton, too, thanks to Trade Union effort, women have for long enjoyed, on the weaving side, a position of equality wellnigh unique.

More than a quarter of all women in Unions belong to the Textiles : there, indeed, they are almost as highly unionised as the men. The average rate—30 per cent.—for the Textiles as a whole is mainly due to the very much higher percentage in weaving. In Wool and Worsted the rate is low, and in Hosiery not high.

Employment in the textiles is skilled. The manipulation and control of costly and complicated machinery require no small intelligence and patience, as well as concentration and manual dexterity. The woman textile worker is proud of her capability and of economic independence.

On the other hand, the Textile trades are low wage trades. The wages of men are low, and in these trades as a whole the wages of women even lower. This is not only the case in Britain. It is found in every part of the world. In 1937, a very valuable study of World Conditions in the Textile Industry was made by the International Labour Office. The Report states :

" When the wage situation in the textile industry is compared with that in other industries, textile workers appear, on the whole, to be in a worse position than most workers in other industries in most countries . . ."

Low wages are general and international. So is the fact that industry employs a very high proportion of women : an average of 50 per cent. The proportion is even higher in Italy (75 per cent.), Portugal, Sweden, the U.S.S.R. and Japan ; it is relatively low in the U.S.A.

These general low wage-rates account for the fact that the typical home in the textile towns, both in Lancashire and Yorkshire, is supported by and dependent on a family wage. In a high proportion of cases, the woman worker stays on in the mill when she marries, or, after a brief interval, returns there, if there are children. She carries a double burden, and its weight is obvious to the most casual visitor to a textile town.

Moreover, although relatively to other industries, the ratio of women in Lancashire Trade Unions is high, it is much lower for women than for men, although women outnumber men ; and the Unions are run by men. The loyalty of the women is perfect. They pay their dues. They come out, when they are called. They work heroically, at election times. But their participation is passive, and their sense of responsibility small. Whether or no because of some innate conservatism in Lancashire, the men certainly do not push the women forward. In some branches they function as minor officers, but neither on the central committee of the Cardroom Amalgamation nor of the Weavers Association has a woman ever sat, although in both these great Unions the women members are in the majority. There is only very rarely a woman in the delegations sent to Trade Union Congress year by year by the Textile Unions. In this and other respects, conditions in this great group of industries present, to anyone who believes strongly both in Trade Unionism and in women, a formidable challenge.

In the economic history of Great Britain, the importance of wool is older than that of cotton. The woollen industry was strongly established, notably in the West of England, before the Industrial Revolution. But the fortunes of Yorkshire, as of Lancashire, were transformed by the discovery of steam-power. For the best part of a century, it came to seem natural, and even inevitable and right, that raw material should be transported across leagues of sea to be worked by skilled fingers in the north of England into fabrics, then sent forth anew across the seas to clothe the peoples living as far off as the distant East. The drive to work and wealth was tremendous. There was of course a grim and terrible side to the swift enrichment the new power made possible ; the towns that were flung up, carelessly, with a total indifference to light, to sanitation, to amenities even of the simplest type, on the sides of the deep valleys through which coursed the precious water-power, blotted out the beauties of the countryside, as the " dark, Satanic mills " they served and surrounded blotted out happiness and denied free growth to the men, women and little children who toiled within them, and suffered things of which, now, we can hardly bear to read. But England grew rich ; Lancashire and Yorkshire were making it rich, and knew a queer, deep pride in the fact.

II. COTTON

This was specially true of Lancashire. On cotton, the Empire rose. " What Manchester thinks to-day, England thinks to-morrow " ; indeed, the free trade under which the vast, new wealth developed so fast was, on the continent of Europe, known as the Manchester system.

No break came in the abounding prosperity of the prosperous until the American Civil War. Then, the fires that slumbered hidden behind the taciturnity of the Lancashire mill-worker were suddenly and splendidly revealed. They were ready to risk all to save others, far away, from slavery. The view of the millowners was given in the jingle of the day :

> Though with the North we sympathise,
> It must not be forgotten
> That with the South we've stronger ties
> Which are composed of cotton,
> Whereof our imports run into
> A toll of many figures ;
> And where would all these imports be
> Without the toil of niggers ?

Far different was the outlook of the mill-workers. To them, those imports meant their livelihood ; but, as so often, they could see a great issue more clearly than their " masters ". No mere materialists, these gritty folk ; they knew what slavery was ; they were for Lincoln and freedom, no matter if it meant, as it did, hard times.

For three-quarters of a century, exports of cotton manufactured goods were the backbone of British foreign trade ; the most important element in Britain's economic predominance. Even before the 1914 war, however, there was a change and, for Lancashire, an ominous change. Competition was growing ; the European and American textile industries were growing ; in the Far East, indigenous industry was growing, notably in Japan. Then war brought to cotton workers a period of hardship as severe as that they had known at the time of the American Civil War. As is stated in the Report of the Cotton Control Board :

> The trade was called upon to suffer, like a non-combatant, from the blows of foe and friend alike ; once again, a patient endurance was the supreme contribution it could render to the cause it had at heart. . . . Though, at one time, the production of the principal section of the industry was cut down to less than 40 per cent. of its normal, the cotton operatives contributed throughout an element of steadiness to the national temper.

Next, and not less serious in its effects on the future well-being of the industry and above all of the workers in it, was the financial frenzy which marked the brief and false post-war boom. A heavy price is still being paid for this unreal and perilous phase of superficial prosperity, during which mills changed hands at inflated prices and cotton shares soared to fantastic levels. It masked, most dangerously, the fact, only too patent when the spurt collapsed, that a change had taken place in the outlook for Lancashire, and one that was likely to be permanent. In the new factories of Japan, of India, and of China, an exploitation of cheap labour like that Lancashire had endured in the early decades of the Industrial Revolution was backed by modern, rationalised organisation, and selling and marketing systems far more centralised and concentrated than Lancashire's. An epoch was drawing to an end. The last twenty-five years have been years of steadily contracting markets, production and employment.

Internal reorganisation is long overdue. It is necessary, if healthy industry is to survive. But few hope to see Lancashire wholly retrieve the position it enjoyed before the 1914 War ; or a cotton industry affording the volume of employment it did in the past. With an insured working population of well over a million, the volume of employment was in 1912 only 712,000 ; in 1924, 610,000 ; and in 1936, 438,000. Production is now only half what it was before 1914 ; the volume of plant in operation has been reduced by a third. Unemployment and under-employment lay like a blight on the lives of its people until 1940. Wartime needs have produced a change, but one that can hardly be permanent.

Under such conditions, Trade Unionism has had a hard fight. Its history is a proud one. Collective bargaining was firmly established in cotton long before it was won in other great industries, and a system of uniform piece-work price-lists was secured. In the early history of Trade Union Congress, cotton leaders play a prominent part. One section of the trade—the weavers—enjoys the almost unique distinction of having secured for its women workers complete equality with their men colleagues so far as basic rates are concerned. Yet, under the crashing blow of the 1929 slump, the machinery of collective bargaining, that had functioned for nearly a century, was so near collapse that, on the manufacturing side, employers and employed came together in an appeal to the Government of the day to set up some machinery to safeguard agreements. A Trade Board was mooted. Actually, under the Cotton Manufacturing Industry (Temporary Provisions) Act of 1934, another solution was adopted ; statutory force was given to the main piece-work price-lists. Even this, however, could not meet the distress caused by low wages and under-employment. At the end of 1939, the Weavers Association applied to the Conciliation Committee, set up as part of the new arrangements, to fix a minimum wage of 35*s*. To this the Committee agreed ; although the agreement still requires legislative sanction before it can go into effect.

The significance of these facts is plain. A great body of industrially employed women are in a low wage industry, which is also, at the same time, an industry in decline. Let us now look at the pre-war position of women, and interrogate it in more detail.

The Cotton trade proper divides itself between spinning and manufacturing.

On the spinning side, women and girls are in a majority, both in the cardroom and in the principal, but by no means the only Union, the Cardroom Amalgamation. Their work covers all stages in the preparation of the raw cotton, and its spinning on a ring frame—a process universal on the Continent, and in Lancashire gaining ground. Out of some 45,000 members of the Amalgamation, over 36,000 are women ; a considerable proportion are young girls. Wage-rates are low : the women's average is 30*s*., as against 50*s*. for the men.

The better-paid section here is spinning on the mule. This is a craft, and rigidly confined to men. Spinners operate with the aid of piecers, also male.

On the manufacturing side, the workers are divided into a series of separate grades, of which the most important are weavers (men and women) ; overlookers (men only) ; twisters and drawers (mainly men ; a very few women) ; tape sizers (men only) ; warehouse-men (men and women, with a heavy preponderance of men) ; and winders, warpers and reelers (women). Numerically, the most important section on the manu-facturing side is weaving.

Here, organisation is very strong. The Amalgamated Weavers Association (formed in 1884 as an association of thirty-four local unions) had, in 1937, 94,000 members, of whom 75,000 were women. In weaving there is complete equality as between men and women, an equality which has so long been the pride of the textiles. The piece-work price-lists negotiated with the employers, and given legal effect by Parliament, apply to the job of work, irrespective of the sex of the worker who performs it. Here in fact is the great, outstanding example of equal pay in practice : the uniform rate for the job. There is no other group of working women of comparable dimensions to whom this applies.

It is, indeed, this fact that makes the figures of women's earnings perturbing and perplexing. Throughout the textiles, in manufacturing as in spinning, the average all-over wage of the women is lower than the men's. Owing, however, to the wide differences that separate the various sections, general average figures mean little. On the manufacturing side there is a strong and long tradition of organisation, backed by equal rates in the premier section. Nevertheless, even in weaving, the average woman's wage is lower : the proportion of women in the lower wage sections is larger : and in every section, up to the most highly paid—that on automatic looms—the woman earns less than the man.

For fully employed workers on ordinary looms, the average wage on full working is 41s. 10d. for a man, 36s. 7d. for a woman. When the figures for four-loom weavers (the majority) are taken, the result is no different. Men earned 40s. 3d. ; women, 37s. 9½d. in a full week. In each group, from one loom to eight, the discrepancy reappears, to the disadvantage of the woman. These are normal (1937) rates.

The same picture is seen when one looks at the distribution of workers as between the relatively well- and the relatively ill-paid groups. Of fully employed adult male weavers, 24·8 per cent. earned less than 35*s*. a week, in 1937 ; the proportion of fully employed adult female weavers earning less than 35*s*. was 45·3. Of under-employed adult weavers, the proportion earning less than 35*s*. was, for men, 62·3 ; for women, 76·4 per cent.

The numbers of automatic looms are as yet small, but they are fairly evenly distributed as between men and women. Here, the earnings vary as between 51*s*. 11*d*. for men, and 40*s*. 1*d*. for women.

These figures are based on the results of a special Census of weavers' earnings, taken first on a day in 1936, and again, on a day in 1937, by the Weavers Association. The day in 1937 was, as it happened, in a relatively good week ; a week, that is to say, with a minimum of under-employment, which is the special curse of the weaver, who then has to stay all day in the mill although, since he tends only one or two, instead of four or six looms, he brings home at the end of a full week only half a week's wages or less. The results of the Census have been carefully weighed and analysed in a monograph published for Manchester University, in 1937, the work of a lecturer in the department of Economics, Mr. E. M. Gray. The special purpose of the inquiry, and of the monograph, was related to the great controversy that has racked Lancashire ever since the depression settled in—the so-called " more looms " controversy : the introduction there of the Northrop or other automatic looms.

Automatic looms have been installed on a considerable scale in the U.S.A. and elsewhere ; but in Lancashire, up to 1937, only to some 5 per cent., although the system is growing. Mr. Gray remarks on the figures for automatic loom workers, that " the most striking result is the difference in the earnings of men and women " ; and devotes some space to a suggestive attempt to analyse the causes. Men, on the whole, organise their work better. They can better support the large amount of walking that is involved in tending a high number of looms. They are more ambitious. Since there are no uniform rates as yet for automatic looms, the employer can, and does, beat the woman down. In so far as she does not, and the man does, work on a two-shift system, he can say that his costs are higher where women are employed.

Nevertheless, the puzzling fact remains that equal piece-work price-lists have not, for women weavers on a normal number of looms, secured actual equality of earnings. Some part of the explanation doubtless lies in the fact that a large number of the women in the mill are doing a double job ; they are at once wage-earners and home makers. In the textiles the proportion of occupied women in the higher age-groups is much larger than for occupied men in general. For women generally, the ages of highest occupation, in the Census use of that term, are 18–20 and 20–24 : in the textiles, the largest group is that between 35 and 44. From a high figure at 21–24, there is a slight drop for 25–29 ; another drop, a little more marked, for 30–34 ; then, a rise for 35–44. Even at the age-group 45–54, the figure is still high ; a tenth of all the occupied women of that age are in the textiles.

Women at Work

AGE DISTRIBUTION OF OCCUPIED WOMEN

Age Group					All Women	Women in Textiles
14–15	.	.	.	.	316,352	21,338
16–17	.	.	.	.	532,175	40,989
18–20	.	.	.	.	831,756	71,458
21–24	.	.	.	.	941,157	94,664
25–29	.	.	.	.	737,042	91,701
30–34	.	.	.	.	480,097	69,754
35–40	.	.	.	.	554,385	55,957
45–54	.	.	.	.	204,553	16,794

A special census taken in 1929 and 1931 showed that of unemployed women in Lancashire, 60 per cent. in 1929 and 55 per cent. in 1931 were married. In some centres the figures were even higher ; in Blackburn it was over 70 per cent. in 1929. Again, in 1929, of the names on the live register of the Employment Exchanges, 32,237 were married, 21,201 single ; in 1931, when the numbers had almost trebled, the distribution was still 87,630 married to 70,160 single women.

The reason of this continuous employment is, of course, economic : the low average wage of the textile worker compels the woman to stay in work, or to return to it, if she has left on marriage, when there are children to support. The proportion of married women in the textiles generally is high ; it is especially high in weaving and hosiery.

As stated in the *Industrial Survey of Lancashire* issued by the Board of Trade in 1929, it is characteristic of the textile industry to rely on a family wage : a joint income to which the wife and the other female members of the family are contributors.

This carries its serious social consequences. The high infantile mortality rate is notorious and tragic. Moreover, " Lancashire women ", said one of them, not with bitterness, but as one stating an obvious fact,

" are beasts of burden." This over-driven, over-burdened condition reacts on industrial push and efficiency ; it reacts, too, on Trade Union membership. Women are too tired to take a keen interest in the Branch meeting. Even the Weavers Association, with its 75,000 women and 19,000 men, only occasionally sends a woman delegate to the Trade Union Congress : in all the Cotton Unions, there is only one woman Branch Secretary.

III. WOOL AND WORSTED

Wool is older than cotton as a staple British manufacture. Before the Industrial Revolution, the woollen and worsted industry was by a long way the most important British industry. Widely scattered, its main centres were in the West of England, in East Anglia, in the West Riding of Yorkshire and south Scotland. Women as well as men were, traditionally engaged in the spinning and weaving of wool as of cotton.

When steam-power created the new factories, there was loom smashing in Yorkshire as in Lancashire ; and the workers of both took part in the defeated struggles of those days to form Unions. The Yorkshire workers played a big part in the Chartist Movement. Conditions in the wool and worsted mills were black, as were those in the cotton mills, for men, for women and for small children.

Individualism is as strong in Yorkshire as in Lancashire ; and since the days of mechanical power, it is in Yorkshire that the industry has been mainly concentrated, although there are still important centres in the West and in Scotland. Organisation, whether on the employing side or on that of the workers, was, however, until the time of the 1914 War, much less concentrated here than in Lancashire. Where Unions existed they were, in the main, small and localised.

Although wool textiles are conveniently treated, in the main, as one industry, there are and always have been big differences in the materials used, technical operations, finished product, and type of industrial organisation, between the worsted and the woollen sides. In the worsted industry, the practice always has been, and still is, for the individual firm to concentrate on special processes ; small local craft Unions could and did deal with relatively small firms. On the woollen side, where the firms are larger, the work is, on the whole, less skilled ; on this side, women heavily outnumber men. Before the 1914 War, weavers in Leeds and Bradford were overwhelmingly women, and young women at that. In worsted, up to 1921, 34 per cent. of the workers were adult males ; the rest being women and juveniles. The proportion of women relative to men has grown. At the same time, all the skilled and craft operations, and all the grades of overlooker and foremen, are, on both sides, reserved for men. On the woollen side, though there are a large number of small firms, with small labour forces, the majority of the workers are employed in large concerns ; 75 per cent., for instance, work within a twenty-mile radius of Bradford.

General conditions in Yorkshire, and especially in the Bradford area, have helped to keep wages low, especially women's wages. Here again we meet the " family wage ", although in form rather different from that in which it is found in Lancashire. Thus Mr. F. Blooman, in his instructive book on the *Industrial Organisation of the Woollen and Worsted Industries*, notes that in Leeds and

Bradford and other West Riding centres, " great advantage " for the employer " is derived from the fact that the heavy industries—coal mining and engineering —there give employment to large numbers of men " : since " the average family earnings tend to be high while labour costs tend to be low ". In other words, the poorly paid employment of the woman as weaver or spinner ekes out the wages of the man in the heavy trades.

Trade Unionism in wool textiles has suffered both from the sectionalism of the trade and, in more recent years, from the slump in exports. Under-employment lies like a curse on wool, as it does on cotton. Only in quite recent years, moreover, has there been any consolidation of Union forces.

By 1881, the (Huddersfield) General Union of Weavers and Textile Workers was the leading Union on the weaving side. But the 1914–18 War, with Government control over the industry, compelled the different sections to get together—at first for the purpose of resisting the extension of insurance. In 1922, the Huddersfield Union amalgamated with the National Society of Dyers and two other Unions, to form the National Union of Textile Workers. In 1936, when the industry began to revive from the worst effects of the slump, another amalgamation took place ; this time between the National Union of Textile Workers, the Amalgamated Society of Dyers, Finishers and Kindred Trades and the Operative Bleachers' (Bolton Amalgamation) to form the present major Union in the wool industry, the National Union of Dyers, Bleachers and Textile Workers. This Union now has a membership of 42,040 men and 33,952 women. In 1917 the National Association of Unions in the Textile Trades was formed, comprising some 20 Unions, excepting those of cotton and lace.[1]

These figures may be compared with those given by the Ministry of Labour Gazette of insured workers in the industry in 1929 :

Males aged 16–64	90,000
Females aged 16–64	123,240

The two sets of figures speak for themselves.

In addition to these wool and worsted workers proper, there are some 100,000 more, included under the " Bleaching, Dyeing and Finishing " heading by the Ministry : 67,130 males, and 26,840 females over 16.

It is obvious from these figures that the rate of unionisation of women on the woollen side is very low : 34,000 only, out of some 152,000.

Until after the war of 1914–18, there was no general wage agreement. Indeed there were, before that, very few collective agreements covering even sections of the trade. In 1919, however, wages for adult male and female piece and time workers were, for the first time, fixed to cover the whole of Yorkshire. Before that, conditions had been quite irregular, and rates, in general, low, with wide variations from grade to grade and even from place to place. During the war the whole industry was placed under Government control. When that phase ended, a Joint Industrial Council was set up. In 1919 it secured a 48-hour week and an agreement on wage-rates which gave rises to compensate for the reduction of hours.

In 1925, a dispute in which the workers demanded a rise, and the employers a cut, in wages, led to the first

[1] Since 1918 the National Association of Unions in the Textile Trades has negotiated for all the Unions in the West Riding.

big general strike the industry had known. A Court of Investigation was set up, which granted neither the rise nor the cut. In 1927, the employers denounced the agreement ; the Joint Industrial Council disappeared ; and, from 1929 on, there was a general wage-cutting campaign, which helped to bring about a heavy slump in Trade Union membership. Between 1927 and 1936 there were no operative collective wage agreements. Indeed wages in certain sections fell so low that the worsted spinning workers asked for a Trade Board. The Board of Inquiry set up as the result of pressure from the Unions recommended, however, that both sides should endeavour to improve their organisation, with a view to the observance of collective agreements. Union amalgamation has helped substantially in this direction. A Wages Agreement is operative, under which basic rates for time and piece workers, and cost-of-living bonus additions under a sliding scale, are fixed.

These rates show the usual discrepancies between men and women. Thus, the basic rate for male workers is 32s. ; that for females, 20s. ; with a minimum for males of 47s. 3d. and for females of 27s. 6d. For piece workers the minimum rate is, for males 32s. and for females, 19s. Under the operation of the cost-of-living sliding scale (January, 1940) the rates, per week of 48 hours, are as follows :

Age				MALES				FEMALES		
				Base Rate		Full Wage		Base Rate		Full Wage
14	.	.	.	10	0	17	5	8	0	13 11
15	.	.	.	11	6	20	0	10	0	17 5
16	.	.	.	13	0	22	7	12	0	20 11
16½	.	.	.	14	6	25	3	13	0	22 7
17	.	.	.	16	0	27	10	14	6	25 3
17½	.	.	.	17	6	30	5	16	6	28 9
18	.	.	.	22	0	38	3	20	0	34 10

Women at Work

IV. HOSIERY

The early days of the hosiery trades showed the domestic system at its worst. Conditions were indeed so wretched that it can be said that the slow change-over to the factory, which took the best part of a half-century to work out, was, on the whole, of advantage to the workers.

The industry has seen a great expansion in recent years, registered in the volume of employment. Always an industry in which women predominated, it employed in 1876, some 5,000 : by 1890, this had risen to 15,630 and by 1907 to 30,000, with the addition of some 25,000 outworkers. In 1930, there were 84,000 women and 23,000 men employed in factories. The evil of home-work has been steadily eliminated ; the other great evil—the excessive employment of young persons —remains. Over 20 per cent. of all the workers are under 18.

On piece-work—the normal system of payment— the average wage, as estimated by the Ministry of Labour, was round about 54s. 8d. for a man and 30s. 3d. for a woman. Mr. F. A. Wells of the University of Nottingham, in his careful study of the industry, says :

" Despite the long tradition of Trade Unionism in the hosiery trade, the movement is not at all strong. The main reason for that weakness is, of course, the large proportion of women workers." Of workers over 18, about 25 per cent. are organised. The English workers are grouped in four main Unions, with centres in Nottingham, Leicester, Ilkeston and Hinckley ; they cover some 14,000 women and 4,000 men.

A Brief Survey of Certain Major Employments

V. CLOTHING

In the group of trades centred in the garment industry, including to-day tailoring in all its branches, from bespoke to mass-production goods, as well as dressmaking and millinery, some half a million workers are employed. Women outnumber men among them, as 3 to 1.

Fifty years ago, the clothing trades covered the widest range of difference in working conditions to be found anywhere. At one end was the tailor, a skilled craftsman, with high and justified pride in his skill. The skilled tailors are among the pioneers of Trade Unionism; although even they had a hard fight to win recognition. The United Operative Tailors belonged to Robert Owen's Grand National Consolidated Trades Union. Although it was smashed, by 1860 the London United Society of Tailors had risen again; soon, too, a National Amalgamation existed, strong enough to lay down a time " log " or rate, and win a 57-hour week. The latter was not really effective : fourteen-, eighteen-, even twenty-hour days were being worked. In some fascinating Recollections contributed to the Union organ, *The Tailor and Garment Worker*, Mrs. Agnes Flynn, after a lifetime of service, recalled these black days, including the arrest of her father for being concerned in a strike of London tailors ; and the culmination of the efforts by early leaders of the Tailors, in Manchester, in the first meeting of the Trades Union Congress there, in 1868. She herself became assistant Secretary to the Union in 1880, at the magnificent salary of twenty pounds a year ; and fought hard to get tailoresses admitted, as was done in 1894. In 1919, the first woman member of the

Union executive appeared in the person of Florence Edwards.

During the larger part of the period covered by Mrs. Flynn's recollections, the skilled tailors were constantly up against the competition of contractors. They represented the other end of the industry's scale : sweated workers, English or immigrant, working under atrocious conditions and vilely underpaid. When Mrs. Webb investigated the London tailoring trades, she found that a shilling a day was as much as a quick worker could bring home at the end of an intolerably long day. Her revelations laid the foundation for the movement for Trade Boards ; indeed there was no possibility of organising the mass of out-workers or those employed by contractors in semi-domestic establishments, until this machinery was set up. Even so the early Trade Board rates were terribly low : 6*d.* an hour for men and 3¾*d.* for women, other than learners ; male learners from 4*s.* 2*d.* to 21*s.* 11*d.* for a fifty-hour week, and females from 3*s.* to 12*s.* 6*d.* a week.

The machine has as thoroughly, though more slowly, transformed the clothing industry as it, earlier, transformed weaving and spinning. The 1914–18 War markedly affected an industry which was kept working at top pressure. The high spotlight during the story of the war years was, naturally, cast on the industries making munitions. But clothing has its part in the story. The manufacture of uniforms created a vast new demand for women workers ; and there were long struggles before these workers won decent rates of pay. It was in these fights that a bright-eyed worker in a Leeds shop suddenly came out as a champion of Unionism. The story of Anne Loughlin is typical and also distinct. She left school at 12, when her mother died, and for the next four years kept house for her father ; on his death she followed her elder sister into the factory and the two of them kept the home going for their younger sisters. After a day's work in the factory, they washed and baked and sewed, for others as well as for their own needs, to bring in extra pennies. In 1912, having already herself joined the Union, she took part in the agitation which got the Trade Board minimum " log " pushed up from 3¼d. to 4d. an hour. When the war brought its toll of heavy work on stiff khaki, she was a leader in organising the girls ; and the Union took her on as organiser at the grand salary of 30s. a week. She led a brilliant strike at Hebden Bridge ; another in the Burberry factory near Reading ; and in Leicester terrorised a great industrial magnate by taking a (perfectly orderly) deputation of a thousand girls right up to the portals of his mansion. Her Union won first 1d. and then 3d. an hour above the Trade Board minimum for its women workers.

To-day Anne Loughlin sits, with Florence Hancock of the Transport Workers, on the General Council of the Trades Union Congress. During the 1914–18 War, women poured into the Union. In 1939, it had 66,807 women members against 23,500 men.

In 1919 it was possible for the first time to win a National Agreement ; shortly after that, many of the existing Unions in both England and Scotland came together to form the National Union of Tailors and Garment Workers. The amalgamation was not completed until the old A.S.T. joined in 1931 and the United Ladies' Tailors in 1938. It is now able to speak as the sole National Union in the industry. Under the agreements it has secured, a 48-hour week has been established ; holidays with pay were granted ; and minimum rates were fixed throughout the range of processes. The Union, nevertheless, faces very difficult problems, in the progress of mechanisation. Mechanisation is making garment-making a mass-production industry ; it is substituting female machine-minders for male craftsmen.

VI. DISTRIBUTION

An outstanding feature differentiating contemporary working conditions from those of half a century ago is the high relative importance of employment in services, personal or other, as contrasted with straight industrial work. This is striking, even if personal service—covering domestic service, hotel and restaurant employment and nursing—be left out of the picture, and the aspect taken is that of the distribution of goods as contrasted with their production. When the transport and distribution of goods, in their various forms, are taken together, they are seen to occupy a high, and constantly increasing, proportion of the workers of the country, its women as well as its men.

In straight transport women are, in peace-time, not engaged in any large numbers. Distribution, however, takes a very large body of working women. Of organised women, the largest block are, of course, in the Textile trades (including garment-making) ; the next largest block are in the Distributive trades ; that is, in the main, in shops. Two great Unions, the National Union of Distributive and Allied Workers, with over 54,000 women in 1939, and the National Union of Shop Assistants, with over 26,000 in the same year, account for over 80,000 women Trade Unionists. There have, from time to time, been projects for the amalgamation of the Unions, sponsored by their leaders ; so far, they have not been carried through, although no really clear line divides their membership, and there is close co-operation and something like a common fighting policy.

The history of organisation in the distributive trades is a tremendous tribute to the power of the Trade Union idea. In some respects, workers in shops present special difficulties to the organiser. At the time when conditions were worst, class snobbery aggravated these, since the young ladies and gentlemen in their black dresses and coats had to feel superior in status, partly because their working conditions were so very miserable. Half a century ago, the shop worker was wretchedly paid and still more uncomfortably housed. Living-in was the rule in establishments of any size; fines cut into low wages; hours were utterly uncontrolled; radius agreements, preventing the worker from moving, deprived him or her of any personal freedom. These shocking conditions obtained even in large and showy establishments; in the smaller ones there was the widest range of variation, depending altogether on the temperament of the employer; but, in general, living and working conditions were alike bad. In the struggle for the redress of grievances, as for the recognition of the right of the workers to combine, a noble part was played by Sir Charles and Lady Dilke: moreover, distributive workers threw up a whole series of brilliant leaders from their own ranks, men like W. C. Anderson, John Turner, and J. J. Mallon were followed by Joseph Hallsworth, John Jagger and Maurice Hann; women like Mary Macarthur and Margaret Bondfield by Ellen Wilkinson. Also, the strength of the Co-operative movement, after it became unionised and after, during the stress of war, it admitted women, had a powerful, if not always appreciated, effect on private trading conditions.

To-day the work of the two great Unions has secured the operation of collective bargaining over a wide field, and has brought about a notable improvement in the pay and conditions of distributive workers of all grades. On very many points conditions lag very far behind the desires of the Unions. There is no legal limitation of hours. Large London and provincial concerns observe a 48-hour week, or less ; they give a regular Saturday half-day off. But in thousands of smaller establishments, in the suburbs, in the country, where the half-day is taken during the week, it is offset by terribly long hours on Saturday, as on every other day of the week in many smaller shops and concerns. The steady demand of the Shop Assistants Union for the establishment of a Trade Board is the register of the evils which the Unions still fight. A Grocery and Provision Board was in fact set up in 1919, but broke down on the refusal of the employers to fix a rate, and after 1921 ceased to function even in name. The campaign launched by the Shop Assistants in 1935 for membership in the great multiple grocery stores did, however, succeed, both in an immense growth in Union membership and in the establishment of a collective agreement with the biggest group of multiple grocery stores.

The membership of the National Union of Distributive and Allied Workers covers a wide range, including clerks and cashiers, warehousemen and porters, bread, coal and milk deliverers, abattoir employees, dairy workers, road transport workers, and laundry workers, as well as shop employees, whether in commercial or Co-operative employment. Grievances, and substantial grievances, remain, both in the pay, the hours and the working conditions of very many workers : yet when the picture of conditions to-day is set against what it was before the Union had grown to representative strength and the power to speak for the workers, the contrast is striking.

It is not a contrast of material conditions only. The two Unions have given self-respect and a just pride in their calling to thousands of men and women. More, in the fights of the present, as of the past, a real solidarity unites the men and women workers in these trades. Here, certainly, they know that their cause is one.

The National Union of Distributive and Allied Workers has the distinction of charging the same Union contribution-rate to women as to men members : (women represent about 30 per cent. of the total strength) ; its policy, and that of the Shop Assistants, is that of the rate for the job, whether performed by a man or a woman. This ideal is not yet realised ; the collective bargaining actually in force accept differential rates ; but it is the one at which the Unions aim, and one which they will achieve the sooner the more women in the trades are inside and help.

VII. ENGINEERING TRADES

Wartime conditions give a new and special importance to these trades, for women as for men. Even in peace-time, however, there are far more women employed in various engineering branches than is generally realised ; and their numbers have been growing steadily in recent years. Pre-war Ministry of Labour statistics gave over 300,000 women as engaged in the diversified branches of this great industrial section. After all, engineering, in the words of no less an authority than Sir Allan Smith, for many years the leader, and a formidable leader, of the employers, " covers anything from a needle to an anchor ". In most of the range of processes thus grouped, women are employed. Yet the number in Unions is very small ; less than 2 per cent.

The reason for this is not far to seek. The Engineering Unions have for long represented the craft standpoint : they have sought to restrict employment to men who have gone through a certain training ; and they have barred women, as representing the unskilled. Writing in the 'nineties of last century, Mr. and Mrs. Webb, in the original edition of their great *History of Trade Unionism*, placed engineering first among the industries, and the engineering Unions first among the Unions of the country. In every sense, indeed, the engineers were then the aristocrats of the world of labour, and the natural leaders in policy. The great upheaval, of which the historic strike at the London docks was an outstanding incident, brought a new and different type of Union into being. The General Labour Union aimed at taking in all grades of workers, for the general protection of all : and, more concerned with fighting strength than the benefit side of the Union, took in members at low contribution rates. At the same time, changing conditions of production, and above all, mass-production methods, based on automatic and semi-automatic machinery, altered the work of great numbers even inside the engineering shops. The engineers could no longer maintain the old, rigid craft regulations. They could not, unless their numbers were to shrink alarmingly, refuse to admit the semi-skilled, and even, later, unskilled workers, who were pressing into the general Labour Unions. By

1914, they had profoundly modified the conditions of their membership—but only so far as males were concerned. To women the doors of the engineering Unions were barred.

They remained barred, throughout the struggles over dilution and substitution of the 1914–18 War.

Congress records, before the war, and even during its course, again and again show the engineers and the metal trades generally maintaining opposition to women on lines by then entirely dropped by the representatives of other trades. There were, for example, a very large number of women in brassworking ; yet the Union spokesman took the view that " to organise is to recognise ", and therefore refused to organise. The Amalgamated Society of Engineers took the same line. So did the other Engineering Unions.

Yet the women were there, and their numbers grew. They were at the benches ; in the cycle and motor trades ; in the electrical trades ; in telephone making, typewriter and sewing-machine making ; indeed, in these last three branches they outnumbered the males. They were there ; and they were, through their fatal cheapness—especially in the juvenile grades—steadily displacing the craftsmen. The Unions complained of " encroachment " ; the women, meantime, suffered from sweating as severe as in any Trade Board industry.

It was the shocking conditions of the women employed before 1914 that gave force and point to the long struggle of Mary Macarthur and the National Federation of Women Workers to organise them. The vastly increased employment of women, under the new conditions, and their large-scale, if temporary, substitution for skilled men, forced the Amalgamated Society of Engineers, as it then was, to enter into a working alliance with the Federation and the General Labour Unions. They saw that, unless rates were to be knocked to pieces, the substituted women had to be paid at a decent level. Nevertheless, when the war was over, and the men resumed their old places, the policy of the Amalgamated Engineering Union did not change from that of the old A S E. They would not admit women ; even in 1941, they do not admit them.

The attitude of the Union has, of course, not kept women out ; the number of women employed in engineering trades has grown steadily. It has grown, indeed, faster than the number of men.

Numbers of Women in the Engineering Trades

1861 46,000	1914 170,000
1871 58,000	1924 202,000
1901 85,000	1935 251,000
1911 128,000	1939 300,000

When the National Federation of Women Workers became, after 1920, a district of the General and Municipal Workers, the women in engineering—in so far as they are in Unions at all—were taken in by that Union and by the Transport and General Workers. These two Unions, since, have been responsible for negotiations with employers aimed at securing fair rates for women workers. Throughout the years immediately preceding the outbreak of the present war, they strove to this end, with unwearying persistence and faithfulness. A statement issued by the Employers' Federation, in the course of these negotiations, gave some striking figures as to the actual distribution in the shops between various classes of worker, which illustrate the process of breaking-up and "de-skilling" jobs, which the engineers will vainly strive to resist, so long as they exclude women.

A Brief Survey of Certain Major Employments

PROPORTION OF WORKERS IN DIFFERENT CATEGORIES

	Percentage in 1928	Percentage in 1935
Skilled	34·1	31·6
Semi-skilled	20·7	20·9
Labourers	13	10·7
Apprentices	7·8	7·5
Youths	9	9·3
Females	7·7	11·4

This notable increase in the proportion of women is reflected in the figures of the 1931 Census, which showed an increase of 72,000 in the number of women in the metal-working industries, against an increase of only 1,000 in the case of men.

The years 1930–5, up to the belated beginning in 1935 of the re-armament programme, showed an increase in the employment of men of only 7 per cent. : the employment of women, in the same period, rose by 27 per cent. The following table shows the number of women employed in 1924 and in 1933; and their distribution, locally.

District	1924		1933	
	Women	Girls	Women	Girls
London Division	33,680	7,490	55,470	8,200
Eastern ,,	77,330	1,430	13,730	2,160
Western ,,	4,040	630	5,150	620
Midlands ,,	78,480	13,000	91,020	13,680
N. Eastern ,,	17,170	3,020	19,460	3,970
N. Western ,,	19,150	3,760	22,750	3,240
Scotland ,,	9,800	1,490	9,220	1,010
Wales ,,	1,180	310	1,530	450
Totals	170,830	31,130	218,330	33,330
Grand Total	201,960		251,660	

Between 1933 and 1939, this proportionate increase went on.

In the autumn of 1938, an application for an advance of wages was made, on behalf of women, by the National Union of Municipal and General Workers. Since the post-war slump, they had only had their wages increased by 2s. against 10s. for men.

At that date there were some 60,000 women in General Engineering ; 26,000 in cycles and aircraft production ; 76,000 in electrical cables ; and some 95,000 in " other metals ". In all these groups their number was rising ; in brass and allied trades, they were stable. Throughout, the basic rates for women were very low : 4d. an hour on piece-work, which was actually below the Trade Boards' average. For the two main classes of women workers in the industry, average earnings were no more than 30s. and 26s. per week. The Union urged, and the employers did not contest the view, that the work was increasing not only in quantity (under the ruthless pressure on the workers of the Bedaux and point systems) but in responsibility, skill and technique required. After long discussions, however, the utmost that could be secured at this stage was a consolidated rate of 28s. for girls under 18, and of 32s. for adults.

War demands, of course, have wholly changed this picture. Employers, faced with a growing dependence on female labour, have been compelled to concede to a rate for the job, for women as for men, after training. Long and patient negotiations, conducted on behalf of the women by the National Union of General and Municipal Workers and the Transport Workers and other Unions resulted in May 1940 in the signature of terms by the employers which give women rates and conditions far better than were achieved in 1914–18.

Women brought in to take men's places are regarded as temporarily employed, and therefore serve a probationary period, in three stages, at the end of which they receive the basic rate and the bonus appropriate to the men they replace ; in other words, they receive the Trade Union rate for the job—man's pay for the man's job.

By the end of 1940, Mr. Ernest Bevin, as Minister of Labour, announced plans for absorbing half a million women into munitions production, based on a preliminary training for eight weeks, on terms practically the same as those for men undergoing training. Inside the Ministry, moreover, women have been appointed to responsible positions to watch over the maintenance of the conditions laid down.

The extent to which their great advance, won by Trade Union action, can be made secure, and can be made to cover all the women engaged on engineering processes, in the widest sense, now and for the future, depends on the women themselves. If they come inside the Unions which have been fighting their battles, and will go on fighting them—the National Union of General and Municipal Workers and the Transport and General Workers Union—they can help, and that powerfully, to hold what has been granted. In doing that, they will be fighting the battle of the men, as well as their own, both now and in the future.

VIII. BOOT AND SHOE TRADES

In these trades Trade Unionism has a long history. More than a century ago, there were numerous small craft associations. When the present National Union was founded in the 'seventies, it consisted of a large number of local associations and branches, many of them pretty independent. The vigour of these associations is remarkable, in view of the fact that at that time the work was still done in domestic workshops and the homes of the workers. Payment was entirely on a piece-work basis.

In conciliation and arbitration procedures, the Union has been a pioneer : the first General Secretary worked out a plan for these. In the 'eighties, however, the employers were strongly hostile to the Union ; they refused to meet it on a national footing. Despite this hostility, the Union grew. In 1892, the employers, after threatening a general lock-out, agreed to a conference and at that conference a national agreement was reached.

Two years later, there was a fresh attempt to break the Union. The employers declared a lock-out and it lasted for six weeks. The workers stood together splendidly. In the end, terms of settlement were reached which have since formed the steady basis for working conditions in the industry. A remarkable feature of the settlement of 1895 was the establishment of a joint Guarantee Fund, administered by trustees, out of which damages might be paid to either side breaking the terms. Since 1895, there has, in fact, been no strike and no lock-out. Subsequent revisions of the Terms of Settlement, which is the charter of the industry, have established a 45-hour week and agreed minimum rates for various classes of workers. Thus, under the heading " Classification of female labour ", it is stated :

It is undesirable that females should be employed amongst male operatives in the Clicking, Press, Lasting and Finishing Departments, in which male labour is now almost exclusively employed. Where females are so employed, they shall receive the wage rates appropriate to males doing similar work.

The minimum rates for females are over 60 per cent. of the male rates.

The Agreement is worked through local conciliation and arbitration Boards, on whom falls the main responsibility of fixing piece-work prices. A high place among the seventy branches is occupied by one in Leicester entirely composed of women, with a woman president and four full-time women officers. The Union in 1939 had 31,000 women to 56,000 men members. Mechanisation has advanced fast in the industry, and is still advancing. Between 1907 and 1938, output per operative increased over 66 per cent.

IX. PRINTING

In 1939, two great Unions, the National Society of Operative Printers and Assistants and the National Union of Printing, Bookbinding and Paper Workers, included women in their delegates to Congress. They covered between them 61,000 men and 37,000 women. These two Unions have done an immense amount to improve conditions for both sexes and for all grades, including typists, in newspaper offices. A small society of women employed in the Bookbinding and Printing Trades carries on the tradition of Emma Patterson. On the other hand, the Compositors, both in London and the Provinces, exclude women.

X. POTTERY

As far back as 1831, under the inspiration of Robert Owen, tremendous efforts were made to form a national organisation for the pottery trades. Then and since, there were great difficulties, partly because, outside the famous Five Towns Arnold Bennett made famous, the industry is very widely dispersed.

The war of 1914–18 was a big, though not a wholly beneficial landmark in the history of the trade. Great numbers of women were then drafted in ; and since, women have outnumbered men : in 1939, they outnumbered them in the Union by 14,392 to 8,583. The National Union has a woman organiser.

XI. CLERKS

In the grouped list of Unions affiliated to the Trades Union Congress, Category 16—Non-Manual Workers —is followed by 17, General Workers. As a matter of fact, a very large number of clerks, especially women clerks and typists, are, like the " miscellaneous " workers in industry, in either the General and Municipal Workers or the Transport Workers Unions.

By and large, however, clerks are very little organised. A large proportion of them work in small offices or concerns. Not a few still hug a certain class superiority, to offset their miserable pay. They have proved hard to get into Unions and harder to keep there. This applies equally to the male and female clerk. Yet efforts to organise them are of long standing : as is natural when it is remembered that the clerical group covers between a million and a quarter and a million and a half workers.

The strongest single Union of clerical workers is the Railway Clerks Association—a very strong organisation. Thirty years ago there were few women employed even in the offices of the railway companies. Moreover, the conditions under which the men clerks were then employed were very bad. Wages were low, hours practically unrestricted, overtime and Sunday duty not paid for. Worst of all, there was no machinery of any sort for getting these or other grievances considered or adjusted.

It was from these conditions and needs that the Railway Clerks Association was born in 1897. It has been from the first an " all grades " association, and takes in clerks, station-masters and agents, inspectors and technical staff. Women came in in considerable numbers only after the outbreak of war in 1914 ; and they came into the Union from the start on equal terms with the men ; although into the Railway service on very much 'inferior terms.

Great difficulties were put in their way by various Railway Companies, and there were many cases of definite victimisation of women who joined the Union. Nevertheless, they did join ; and it was through Union action that scales of pay were fixed, although these varied as between the different Companies, were always lower than the men's, and did not, up to the end of war, carry equal cost-of-living bonuses : they were, in fact, paid less than half the rates given to men, while their general conditions were highly unsatisfactory.

It was, of course, not till after the Railway strike of 1919 that full recognition was won by the Unions ; and not until August, 1920, that the Railway Clerks Association was able to secure an agreement covering the position of women and girl clerks. A year later, under the Railways Act, orderly negotiating machinery was set up under persistent pressure from the Union. The scale for women, which was won in 1920, included a basic rate of 30s. a week at 18, rising to 60s., with annual increment and Special Class rates ; the same rates and conditions as the men for overtime and Sunday duty ; extra London allowance.

Inequalities remain. The scope of promotion is limited. The women's scale remains lower than the men's. Their position as regards superannuation falls short of what the Union struggles to win for them. At the same time, they are infinitely better off than they could be without a Union which treats them as members on a complete equality ; is, in its constitution and all arrangements, fully democratic ; and secures them, to-day, a whole range of benefits, from Convalescence and Retirement to Unemployment. They are vastly better off than their fellows in commercial clerical employment. In 1939, the Railway Clerks Association, with over 57,000 male members, had 6,350 women. There is a woman member of the Executive.

There are also some 21,000 women members of the National Union of Railwaymen, mainly employed in the Hotel services connected with the various railways.

There are more women in the Railway Clerks Association than in the National Union of Clerks, which, in 1939, had 5,509 women to 8,708 men members : a big falling off from the much larger numbers for the 1914–18 years. An active and energetic all-women Clerical Union—the Association of Women Clerks and Secretaries, has 2,500 members. Its secretary, Miss B. A. Godwin, is one of the very live wires in the women's Trade Union movement.

XII. DOMESTIC SERVICE

More than a million and a half women are normally employed in domestic service. Scattered, and for the most part isolated, since the majority of them are

" generals " in households where only one maid is kept, these are, obviously, among the most difficult workers in the country to organise. Efforts have often been made by ardent spirits, both inside and out, only to peter out after a brief struggle. The fact that domestic servants are still outside the scope of the Insurance Acts is yet another handicap. No lasting organisation was built until 1937, when the General Council of the Trade Union Congress took the matter in hand.

The need for organising this very large block of employed women—more than a quarter of the whole number of working women—had long been plain, both from the point of view of domestic workers themselves, and from that of their fellow-workers, whether men or women. But, without help from outside towards organisation and finance, nothing lasting could be achieved. These were the arguments that convinced the Council. In July, 1937, a National Union was founded, with its headquarters at Transport House, and a very capable organiser in Beatrice Bezzant, herself an ex-domestic worker. The objects of the Union, as embodied in the Constitution, are :

(1) to regulate the conditions of employment and the rates of pay of domestic workers of either sex ;

(2) to raise and maintain funds for these purposes and for the relief of members when victimised or in distress, and to assist members in obtaining suitable employment ;

(3) to provide legal aid for members in connection with their employment, covering dismissals without notice, breach of contract, accidents at work, workmen's compensation, Employers' Liability, libel and slander ;

(4) to advance the economic and social interests of its members in all possible ways ;

(5) to promote friendly relations and co-operation between the Union and other Trade Union organisations.

Membership is open to any person, of either sex, whose employment is private domestic work. The Union drafted a Charter, in which the essential point is the regulation of conditions of work, notably in relation to hours, the most serious grievance of the domestic worker. The revolution that has taken place in the average kitchen—the gas or electric cooker ; the fitted bathroom, the vacuum cleaner, etc.—and in the average house, in the last quarter of a century, has abolished much of the sheer drudgery that used to be part of domestic employment. But it has not, so far, availed to limit hours of work. These unlimited and uncertain hours, with the absence of personal freedom they carry with them, explain the fact that workers are, to-day, in the strong position given by a demand in excess of supply. It also explains the general antipathy among men and women for an occupation not in itself uncongenial and their tendency to regard it as an " inferior " line of employment. Long hours coupled with lack of freedom make it difficult for domestic workers to take part in social, educational or political activities. They also limit their chances of marriage. Although it is generally supposed that a girl " in service " will always marry, sooner or later, in actual fact domestic service has a lower marriage rate than any other industrial or professional group.

By the end of a year, the Union had over 1,200 members, two-thirds of them in the Greater London area, which was divided into fourteen branch districts ; there were also by then four provincial branches. Growth cannot, in the very nature of the case, be rapid ; but the better type of employer is, says the Union's secretary, " as anxious as the worker to improve conditions ". The Union will, here as elsewhere, help the good employer to cope with the bad, by establishing standards that all must observe.

The Union, as has been stated, is open to workers of either sex. For those under 16 there is no entrance fee, and the contribution is one penny per week ; for those between 16 and 18, the entrance fee is 3*d*., and the contribution rate 2*d*. a week ; for those over 18, the entrance fee is 6*d*., and the weekly contribution 4*d*. The Union provides legal assistance, covering dismissal without notice, compensation, breach of contract, accidents while at work, as well as Employers' Liability, libel and slander. In the first year over £80 was reclaimed for members, in sums ranging from 2*s*. 3*d*. to £7. There are various additional benefits, including hostel and holiday benefit.

CHAPTER IX

PAYMENT

" If you take a man off a machine and put a woman in his place, there is no reason at all why that woman should not have the same rate as the man gets."

" That is where we differ."

This passage occurred at a meeting, late in 1939, between the Engineering Employers Federation and representatives of the General and Municipal Workers Union, speaking on behalf of women in the engineering trades. The spokesman of the Union stated bluntly, " If output is the same, there is no reason why the worker should suffer a penalty because she is wearing skirts instead of trousers."

This is a view now consistently taken by the Unions. On its realisation in action the hopes of the woman worker depend, whether her work is inside the home or outside of it.

It is not the view that, by and large, obtains in practice. Union action has established the principle, in wartime, for certain important groups of women workers who are taking the place of men; and this is a very significant forward step, which may have long consequences. Throughout normal employment, however, the governing word is that of the employer : " That is where we differ." The woman, because she is a woman, is paid a lower rate than the man. The difference varies. In a few occupations, she gets 60 per cent. of the man's rate ; over a far larger range, something under 50 per cent. is considered sufficient.

In October 1938 the Ministry of Labour made an inquiry into earnings, completed in 1940 to determine what the movement had been since the outbreak of war. Forms were sent to all employers of more than ten work people, and to a selection of those with less, in manufacturing industries and the principal non-manufacturing industries. 741,000 employers sent in returns, covering nearly 5,500,000 workers. In July 1940 forms were again sent to the majority of these establishments and to some new ones in the engineering and allied trades : the number of workers covered being appreciably higher than in 1938.

The object of the inquiry was not to show the difference between male and female *rates* ; these rates are not separately given for 1938. But for July 1940 the amounts earned by men and women are returned, together with the percentage increase over October 1938 which the 1940 rates represent for each group.

In this table, workers of all grades in each group are massed together to give average earnings. Some slight adjustment must, no doubt, be made to allow for the fact that a higher proportion of men are on overtime ; and that there are, at any time, a higher proportion of men in the higher grades and by July 1940 this had probably been only slightly affected by wartime conditions. This appropriation of the higher, and higher paid, jobs by men, however, is part of the general problem of women's wages. As they stand, the over-all rates correspond broadly with all previous statistics for women's earnings.

The figures speak for themselves. They show the woman's earnings hovering at or below 50 per cent.

Women at Work

COMPARATIVE EARNINGS OF MEN AND WOMEN
(*Labour Gazette :* Nov. 1940, Dec. 1940)

Employment		*July, 1940*		*Percentage increase over October, 1938*
		s.	*d.*	
Metals, Engineering, Ship-	men	100	3	36·3
building	women	43	11	36·4
Textiles . . .	men	72	10	11·9
	women	36	5	10·4
Clothing (inc. Boots and	men	75	10	32·6
Shoes, Laundries)	women	39	9	25·5
Food, Drink, Tobacco .	men	76	8	16·3
	women	35	10	7·5
Woodworking Trades .	men	77	5	16·1
	women	38	11	16·8
Paper, Printing, etc. .	men	83	10	·6
	women	35	4	4·4
Chemicals . . .	men	89	6	25·6
	women	37	4	14·2
Brick, Pottery and Glass .	men	78	0	23·5
	women	33	0	18·6
Leather, Leather Goods .	men	76	10	19·4
	women	35	11	3·9
Misc. Manufacturing .	men	94	9	36
	women	39	4	23·6

of the man's. Often they are a good deal less, as in Metals, Engineering, Shipbuilding, Printing, Chemicals, Brick, Pottery and Glass, and Miscellaneous Manufacturing. Only in the Textiles are they a little over 50 per cent. of the man's.

Moreover, the picture is repeated in the column showing the percentage advances of July 1940 over October 1938. In Engineering the woman's percentage advance is a little bigger than the man's, although the discrepancy between their earnings remains enormous. In Printing and Paper, where again the discrepancy is great, the improvement over 1938 is very small, but the woman gets a little more, plus 4·4 per cent. against the man's 0·6 per cent. In every other case, the percentage rise in the man's higher earnings is well above the percentage rise in the woman's lower wage.

The table covers manufacturing industry. This, as has been shown, is the best chapter in woman's pay-book. Were it possible to complete the picture, by taking personal service, clerical and casual employment, the demonstration would be heavily underlined. In unorganised employments, the inferiority of the woman's earnings is more marked. Women's wages in women's trades are, as a rule, lower than their earnings where they work side by side with men—since, in the latter case, they often enjoy the protection of Trade Union organisation.

As it stands, the table is sufficient to make the point which no one disputes, because it cannot be disputed ; women who earn in the neighbourhood of 50 per cent. of what men earn count themselves lucky.

This is the broad picture. It is a 90 per cent. picture. Few and far between, in normal times, are the cases where there is established a rate for the job, irrespective of the sex of the worker. These exceptions only show up, in vivid relief, a general rule that women, as such, are paid less.

Since political emancipation the case for a sex rate is not generally stated with explicit bluntness. It is wrapped up in arguments about the lower standard of living of the female of the species ; about her relative independence of family claims ; about the dangers that, if paid the same rate, she will in fact be crowded out of employment. But when each of these arguments has been met and disposed of, a hard core remains, un-affected. Common to all ranges of occupation—manual, industrial, clerical, domestic, professional—is the practice of paying a woman at a lower rate, not on any argument, simply because she is a woman.

Most industries and services have men's rates and women's rates ; and the women's rates are invariably lower. Sex differentiation rules throughout the world of employment, with few exceptions, cotton weaving and certain branches of the boot and shoe trade being the outstanding instances. The characteristic women's trades are low-wage trades. Where men and women work at the same trade, the women are on lower rates, and are confined, as a rule, to the lower ranges of employment.

It is still true, as Mary Macarthur put it, that " Women are badly organised because they are badly paid ". Low payment, absolute and relative, is the governing fact in the position of the woman worker : her economic position, her social position. The great mass are in low-paid lines of work. They are paid in those low lines, and elsewhere, less than men doing the same work. Very few women are in the higher paid lines ; there, too, they are, as a rule, paid less than men.

There are a few cases in which women are treated as workers, not as women workers ; they only throw up in clearer relief the general picture, which is one of inferiority imposed by the employer, and accepted by the woman, although this acceptance, almost universal in the past, is changing fast.

In the entertainment world, in the widest sense, women are paid, like men, a strictly individual rate. Film stars and opera singers, actresses and painters, are not paid less because they are women. On the stage, whether legitimate or variety, and the screen, women happen to be indispensable, and profit by the fact. Throughout the highly individualistic world of the arts, indeed, sex is recognisedly an irrelevant factor in remuneration. The novel by a woman carries the same royalties as the novel by a man. Pictures are not priced by the sex of the painter. The woman virtuoso stands on her achievement.

In politics, again, there is equality at the top. A woman Minister of the Crown is paid a salary fixed without regard to the sex of the person who draws it ; so is a Member of Parliament.

Certain professional associations have or are getting rates fixed which are standard for the job and independent of sex. In the technical field, the fee of doctor, architect, barrister, is neutral.

In scientific research women can and do enjoy genuine equality of opportunity and even of reward, at the top.

Access to the top, where this equality prevails is, however, most strictly restricted. As technician, doctor, teacher, civil servant, a woman is, in theory, free to proceed to the limit of the scale. In practice, she seldom gets there. In business, as in the professions, the share of the " plums " going to women is small indeed. No matter how fully trained she is and how personally competent, she finds that the avenue of promotion is, somehow, limited. The possibility of a woman's holding down a big job simply does not occur to those making higher appointments, when the time comes. Prejudice is always, and often sincerely, denied ; the habit of thinking of competence in male terms adheres. If challenged, the reply comes that " others " would—no doubt foolishly—fail to feel confidence in a woman in this or that place. Regretfully, therefore . . .

This applies to fields in which capacity has already been tested and proved, like education and medicine. The number of women filling high University posts or high medical positions is very small. In law, although they are permitted to practise, the bench remains closed ; in journalism, they edit women's pages, but not the paper and so on . . .

The practice of Government here sets an evil example. Not only are differential rates the rule, throughout the Social Insurance systems ; the Civil Service, both national and municipal, is governed, save for certain technical grades, by sex differentiation in payment. From certain branches, women are excluded altogether (diplomatic and consular service, and posts in service departments) ; where they are admitted, and not " segregated " but doing identical work, they are nevertheless paid different rates. The entrant, whether male or female, passes in through the gate of an anonymous and highly competitive examination, and starts at the same salary. Very soon, however, differential scales come into play ; women proceed by smaller increments to a lower maximum. They are, moreover, under an obligation, not imposed on their male colleagues, to retire on marriage.

The Civil Service practice (defended, to-day, only on the ground that it would cost a lot to equalise rates) reacts on the world outside. In industry and commerce, of course, the picture is much darker. Whether on the productive or the distributive side, women are, on the whole, doing the low-paid and socially inferior jobs. Whereas the man of average ability expects to rise to the higher positions in his own line of work, only the woman of exceptional ability can do so. The number of women in the professions, strictly so called, is of course small in relation to the total volume of women's employment. But the status and pay of women in the professions are important to all women who work : they react upon the conditions of them all. Here the standard is set. The rule is laid down here : the hard rule of lower pay and fewer chances for the woman, because she is a woman.

Throughout the industries and services which occupy the great majority of " gainfully employed " women the rule lays down for women something between 60 and 50 per cent. of the man's rate. This applies where they are working side by side with men. In the so-called " women's trades " the run of rates is low ; the characteristic women's trades are low-wage trades. Moreover, of the great blocks of typical female employment, only teaching and nursing stand out against the general routine background as having compensations in the nature of the work itself. In nursing, the worker can have a positive sense of usefulness and the knowledge of rendering to her fellows a unique and essential service. Nursing can be, and often is, more than an employment ; it is a vocation. Too much advantage has, in the past, been taken of this. To-day, partly as the result of the great changes brought about by the Local Government Act of 1929, conditions in hospitals, general, special and mental, are steadily improving. Very long hours are being reduced ; freedom is greater than it was ; pay is rising slowly under the pressure of a demand for nurses that exceeds the supply. The Trades Union Nurses' Charter would carry this improvement much further.

In teaching, again, women can be and are sustained by the knowledge that their work has both social and intrinsic interest. Here, the vocational element enters

in, to a very large extent. Here, however, the main
lever in bringing about improved conditions, a rising
status, and a strong and enlivening sense of self-respect,
has been organisation : Trade Union action and Trade
Union comradeship.

For the bulk of workers in industrial, clerical, casual
or domestic employment it is not easy to find much
interest in the work as work. It is certainly very
difficult, so long as the worker thinks of herself as an
isolated unit. But a change can come, so soon as she
thinks in terms not of individual, but of group contribution to the needs and service of the community ;
so soon, that is, as she enters into the life of a real
association. And the lift of mood that Trade Unionism, with its corporate life, interest and effort, can
bring is, at the same time, putting into the hand of
every worker the one great lever that can improve
depressed economic conditions. For inequality of payment the one efficient remedy is the acceptance and
operation of the rate for the job : only Trade Union
action can enforce this.

Here the argument, now accepted by Trade Unionists, has been put with incomparable force and point
by a woman whose name must always stand high in
any survey of the services of women, either in Trade
Unionism, or to the real and lasting emancipation of
their own sex, Beatrice Webb. Nothing probably
affected the thinking of the general public about Trade
Unionism to such far-reaching effect as did the two great
studies by her and Sidney Webb, *The History of Trade
Unionism* (1894) and *Industrial Democracy* (1897). With
these two major volumes there stands, like them, in that
it possesses lasting value, the small book by her issued
in August 1918, under the title *The Wages of Men and*

Women : Should they be Equal ?   After more than twenty years, this can still stand as the best statement, not only of the claims of women to equality in remuneration, but of the basis of Trade Union action itself, in so far as it has to do with wage standards.

The origin of the book is this : in August 1918, the Committee on Production made an award giving to women bus-conductors an advance equal to that earlier given to men.   The Committee also stated that the claim they had granted in this industry must apply to women employed elsewhere ;   they advised that a general guiding line should be laid down.   On this the Ministry of Munitions insisted that equal pay would lead to an " unwarrantable increase in national expenditure " ;   and asserted that no pledge of equality of payment had been made in the Treasury Agreement of March 1915.   The Trade Unions, on the other hand, insisted that in this Agreement such a pledge had been given.   The Prime Minister then set up a Committee —The War Cabinet Committee on Women in Industry —to go into the whole matter.   Of the six members, two were women.   The Majority Report held that the Treasury Agreement was not a pledge, but recommended that where men and women were doing the same jobs " pay should be in proportion to efficient output ".   Mrs. Webb, rejecting this ambiguous phrase, wrote a Minority Report, afterwards reprinted in booklet form.   That report contains a clear and cogent statement not only of the case for paying women and men the same wages when they do the same work, but of the principles on which remuneration, whether of men or of women, should be based.   It is, of course, the realisation that those principles are the sheet-anchor of Trade Unionism that has caused the gradual con-

version of the entire Trade Union movement, not to
" equal pay ", which is often a phrase without clear
meaning or content, but to the application to women
as to men of the rate for the job—a guiding-line for
action at once definite and practical.

Mrs. Webb's argument is so important that, since
her booklet is not as familiar as it deserves even, to-day,
to be, it is worth while to summarise here its main lines.
She starts by a very important refusal.   She refuses to
accept the assumption which she finds " perhaps in-
advertently " underlying the Majority Report :   the
assumption that " industry is normally a function of
the male, and that women, like non-adults, are only
to be permitted to work for wages at special hours,
under special supervision, and subject to special
restrictions by the legislature ".   She asserts that consideration of the right relation between the wages of
men and women must deal with both sexes, and
begins, therefore, by examining the principles on which
wages are actually fixed.   In the first half of the
nineteenth century, there was no principle at all ; the
whole thing was left to the " higgling of the market ".
This " higgling " dominated the wages of women to
an even greater degree than those of men, though it
also dominated the wages of non-organised men ; in
either case, the effect was to keep rates down to levels
barely sufficient to maintain existence.   It produced
the morass of sweating.   In resistance to this " higgling
of the market " and its fatal results, there arose—

> An association among wage-earners with a view to the
> substitution of collective bargaining and the determina-
> tion of common minimum conditions applicable to all
> persons employed in a particular grade or at particular
> tasks.

In other words, Trade Unionism and the standard rate—recognised as the minimum to be paid to the person undertaking a particular kind of work. Unhappily, this standard rate for long operated against women, inasmuch as they were kept out of the lines of work and the training for the kinds of work to which it applied. Down to the 1914 War, in fact, there were " over the greater part of the industrial field, men's rates and women's rates."

> It must be said that these contrasted men's rates and women's rates bore no definite proportion to the physiological or mental expenditure of the workers of the two sexes in their several tasks, whether measured by their " efforts and sacrifices " or merely by time. Nor does it appear that the several rates were proportionate to the value of these services.

Taking the view that " the prescription and the resolute enforcement throughout the whole community of minimum conditions of service form the indispensable basis of any decent social order ", Mrs. Webb goes on to say that the minimum must be " equal and in fact identical for persons of either sex ". This is, further, the basis of any efficient system, from the economic point of view. The use of cheap labour to cut rates is uneconomic, as well as socially harmful. It is on maximum production and economic efficiency that she takes her firm stand, in putting the case for the rate for the job. Thus, if women are in fact not up to the work they are doing, there is

> national loss in bribing the employer by permitting him to pay lower wages . . . to get his work done by workers industrially less efficient—whether women or men—so long as any efficient workers for the task required are available. Uneconomic, again, is the exclusion, from

any occupation whatsoever, of persons who prove themselves competent at the work.

This is uneconomic ; it is also a restriction on the liberty of the citizen.

While thus firmly establishing the equality of women as workers, Mrs. Webb rejects the formula " equal pay " as unmeaning. It could work only if there existed universal piece-rates which were at the same time occupational and standard rates for the job. She takes her stand on the rate for the job. In so doing, she faces, quite frankly, the argument that if this is done, women will be pushed out of employment ; and finds little in it. Experience in the textile trades ; in nursing ; in teaching in America, where salaries are the same for women and men ; and in the professions, fails to support such a view.

> In so far as differences for efficiency for particular tasks prove to be generally coincident with differences in sex, there would accordingly tend to be, with uniform rates, a general segregation of sex, men gravitating to the occupational grades in which they were superior to women, and most women to those in which they were superior to men, but with exceptions on both sides for individuals who had peculiar tastes or aptitudes or who were above or below the common run of their sex. There is no reason to regard this result as otherwise than advantageous to the community ; and likewise, in its securing the most advantageous relations between productivity and the efforts and sacrifices involved, to all persons concerned, not less so in the case of the woman than in that of the man.

In her final paragraphs, Mrs. Webb sums up the case. " For the production of commodities and services, women no more constitute a class than do persons of a particular creed or race." The time has come for the removal of

All sex exclusions, and the opening of all posts and vocations to any individuals who are qualified for the work, with the insistence, as minima, on the same qualifications, the same conditions of employment, and the same occupational rates, for all.

The essential principle which should govern all systems of remuneration, whether in private industry or public employment, in manual work as well as in brain work occupations, is that of clearly defined Occupational or Standard Rates, to be prescribed for all persons of like industrial grade ; and whether computed by time or by output, to be settled by collective agreement between representative organisations of employers and the employed ; and enforced, as minima only, on the whole trade or vocation. There is no more reason for such Occupational or Standard Rates being made to differ according to the worker's sex than according to race or creed, weight or height.

This is plain, sound sense. This standpoint is to-day accepted by the overwhelming majority of Unions. It is their aim—the rate for the job. It is, however, an aim that cannot be realised until the proportion of women who are organised is very much higher than it is.

The women who are organised accept or endorse this claim. In so doing they stand for genuine equality : the fair field and no favour, or disfavour, on account of sex. They face, realistically, the possibility, which has so often in the past been used to frighten them, that the establishment of standard rates would contract their chances of employment. They know only too well the disastrous actualities of " cheap labour " ; they believe, and with reason, that in organisation they possess a lever capable of lifting the basic rate to a living minimum. With confidence they call upon their fellow-women to put their strength, too, behind the lever, and so give it effective power.

CHAPTER X

SOME PROBLEMS

No one knew better and faced more realistically than Mary Macarthur the difficulties in the way of organising women. To the full she realised that low payment, though the first and greatest of these, was not in itself the whole story. Very many, indeed most, women are engaged in monotonous and uninteresting work, which lacks entirely the stimulus of responsibility and the zest of possible advance to higher tasks. No paradox is, in fact, more characteristic of the Capitalism system under which we live than the practice of paying workers more in proportion as work grows more interesting and more responsible, and less in proportion as it is disagreeable and dull. From this women suffer acutely.

The reaction on the woman worker of restricted promotion and extremely limited responsibility is depressing ; and the depression extends even to those of them who are inside the Trade Union movement. Idle to burke the fact that, there, they hardly pull their weight. In loyalty they are splendid ; in leadership, weak. This is the case even in the textiles, where women outnumber men in the Union as at the looms. They take but a tepid interest, in the main, in Trade Union business, and are rarely found in executive positions, even in the branches. It is the case even in Unions like the Boot and Shoe and the Shop Assistants, where, again, women work side by side with men, or in the National Union of Distributive and Allied

Workers, where the same is true, and where there is no differentiation in their rate of Union contribution. Outstanding women have played and play their part in the national organisation ; but the average standard of participation in Trade Union business by women members is low.

This fact is closely connected with the actual restrictions on the scope of women in employment. They are only in very rare cases considered for or admitted to supervisory posts. In weaving, for example, there are no women overlookers, and only an occasional woman student appears in a technical school in Lancashire. It is so, throughout. Their work, speaking broadly, gives them little or no practice in the independence, initiative, power to act on their own judgement and habit of responsibility which are required in the Trade Union leader, even in the limited sphere of the branch. On the contrary, the routine nature of their work lowers their spirits and makes them feel of small account. Until recently, moreover, the normal attitude even of the most friendly male colleague has been one of small expectation from them.

The position in the hosiery, weaving, clothing, boot and shoe trades, like that in laundry work, hotel and restaurant service, office cleaning and charing trades, is the more significant in that, here, the stock explanation of the " difficulty " of women from the organiser's point of view cannot be cited. This is, of course, the impermanence of women as workers ; the fact that they expect to leave paid work when they marry. In these occupations a high proportion of women continue in work, even if they marry. In that event, of course, a different trouble presents itself : the married worker has a home to look after when her day in factory, shop or office is done. Small wonder if she does not, in such case, find enough energy over to give to Trade Union business or, indeed, anything else.

To-day the number of homes that depend upon and require the joint earnings of both wife and husband is large, and was, before the war, growing larger : considerable, too, is the number where, owing to the death, desertion or invalidity of the husband, the woman of the house has also got to be its breadwinner, in whole or in part. This double burden on large numbers of women workers on the one hand makes them weak bargainers ; in exceptional need of Trade Union support. On the other, it makes them, inevitably, poor Trade Unionists.

Small wonder that the woman worker, thus encumbered with problems, social as well as economic, is something of a headache to the organiser, who, at the same time, knows that she needs help in more ways than the improvement of her working conditions. From whatever angle her position is considered indeed, it forces the considerer to face far-reaching and fundamental issues, affecting the whole shape of our common existence, and not the industrial shape only. Thus about the married woman worker two schools of thought are in contention : two views are ranged against each other in the minds of thinking women and thinking men : schools and views that are hardly capable of reconciliation without some drastic change in the structure of society as we have it to-day. If justification were needed for a study of the position of the woman worker, it is here. She represents a clear challenge to things as they are. Her happiness and her usefulness are alike bound up with and depend upon a radical change ; she embodies " the question that is also prophecy ".

From this point of view it is worth while to set out the two views, as far as one can without bias in favour of one or the other, on the lines of the two schools of thought that uphold them.

On the one side stand those who hold, broadly, and in the main, that marriage and even child-bearing, while important both to the woman concerned and to society, should nevertheless be regarded as incidental to, and not revolutionary of, the life of woman, as of man. Vitally significant incidents, yes : incidents that belong to the full human development of the human creature, yes : not, however, incidents that should deflect and alter the entire course of personal development and reduce, or elevate, all women to a uniform pattern of experience. Those who take this view deny that matrimony is either physically or emotionally a revolutionary event. The woman of to-day is, they urge, and with force, as tough if not as strong as the male. Does not her longevity prove it ? With proper medical care before and after, the process of child-bearing is no more disturbing than a minor operation. No reason, there, why the woman who wants to go on with work should not do so. Not every mother is, in fact, the best guide or companion for her children ; anyhow, the children soon reach an age when it is not desirable that her interest should be concentrated on them. Home-making is a talent, like another, and by no means found in every woman, just because she is a woman. The community is best served by permitting women, like men, to follow freely their various capacities.

This school can certainly call a formidable array of facts to its support. To begin with, there are more women than men, in the population of Britain. Many women cannot marry. The single women suffer both in work and payment for work, from the unwarranted assumption that marriage will provide for them. On the basis of the 1931 Census, 1½ million women of 35 and over remain unmarried out of a total population at those ages of 9 millions. In other words, one girl in every six must expect to remain single. Of the married, one in five of those between 18 and 24 were actually contributing through paid work to the upkeep of the home ; and one in ten of those between 25 and 44. These hard realities make nonsense, and dangerous nonsense, of any expectation, on the part of employer or worker, that marriage is going to lift from women the obligation to work for wages. From this vain dream she must free herself ; the sooner the better for herself.

The other school of thought does not, and cannot, refuse these economic facts. But, it urges, they do not alter the basic situation. For women over 25, in 90 per cent. of cases, marriage is a career, and both an absorbing and worthwhile career. It is accepted as such by the feelings of most women. On the one hand, the work they do, while in paid employment, is not in fact such that they are sorry to leave it, or such that society is better served by their sticking to it. On the other hand, the work they do in the home can only be done by them, and is intrinsically and socially of higher value and importance. The handful of professional women doing work that interests them, that asks for skill, and is better done because they have experience and practice, represent but a drop in the ocean ; any argument carried over from them to the working woman is false in fact and implication. The expectation that a woman should, normally, while still young, exchange work in shop, factory, office or someone else's house, for work in her own home is, from the standpoint of community, sound and desirable. Social practice should be based on normal, not on exceptional cases. The family home, made by the wife, and based on the earnings of the husband, is, so this school argues, the right and desirable norm. Nature, and not convention or prejudice, has decreed that marriage is for woman an experience different not in degree but in kind from what it is for man. Further, the creation of a home and the bearing and rearing of children represent a major service to the community ; woman is not lowered, but lifted, in the true scale of social values when the duties and functions she and only she can perform are rated high, by the State, by public opinion, and, above all, by herself. Here is a task that takes skill, patience, intelligence, character and experience ; for it, an education as complete as that given to the professional is required. She gains rather than loses in status, on any sound view, when she takes on and sticks to this work, which only she can do. It is, after all, in the home, if anywhere, that men and women enjoy and create the values for the sake of which all work is carried on : to which work is but the means. True of any authentic home, this is outstandingly true of the home where there are children. From the standpoint of the community, there have got to be children, and, if possible, more than one or two of them. The atmosphere of early years matters more in psychological, as in physical development, than anything that comes after. There the Nazis are right, horrible as the conclusions are that they draw from their thesis. Of citizen virtues the family must remain the basis. As for the " right " to go out of the home to work, it is a middle-class illusion. Most women do not, in fact,

share it.   To the married professional woman, or the
civil servant called upon to leave work at the precise
juncture when she is, and is aware of, achieving a
certain mastery over her task, which yields an almost
æsthetic satisfaction, there may be hardship in the
change thus wrought in the fabric of her life.   Few
women engaged in clerical, domestic or industrial
employment care for work, or can be expected to care
for it, for its own sake.   They would much rather work
inside homes of their own.   If they continue at work
after marriage, it is not out of choice that they do so ;
merely out of hard economic necessity.

In both these views there is, plainly, a certain
admixture of what used to be called idealisation, and
is called, in contemporary jargon, " wishful thinking ".
The first view idealises work, and leaves out the
miserably inadequate wages earned.   The second view
idealises conditions in the average home—again, by
leaving out the inadequate wages on which it is sustained.   Although each is a trifle inclined to moralise
about the matter, they agree in asserting a woman's
right to make her own free choice.   They could, if
they chose, go on to agree in stating that few women
have any such opportunity in fact.   They could show
with force and point, too, that she is apt to come off
second-best, all along the line.   Educational chances,
in most families, go to boys rather than girls.   Fewer
girls get secondary schooling ; fewer go to college.
Parents take a more responsible view, when it comes
to employment, of the future of their sons than of their
daughters.   Whether or no this is covered by the view
that girls will, anyhow, " marry in the end ", the fact
remains.   Freedom of choice is certainly very straitly
limited.

The limitation is, in the case of women, partly conventional. In the past, women themselves have accepted and even shared the conventional view that kept them out of all sorts of activities and denied them all sorts of opportunities. They have tended to expect little of themselves, and to be too humble in their claims for scope and occasion, too modest in their taking of responsibility. It is to some extent the fault of women that the status of the home-keeper is low and its tasks assumed to need no training ; that the vocational aspect of nursing, teaching and social work of all kinds, has been exploited is also, to some extent, their fault. It is even, to some extent, the fault of women that their rate of payment and status in work are alike low. Grant, fully, all the special disabilities from which they suffer ; it remains true that they often " fail to see the point " of belonging to a Union, which could help them immensely ; and if, inside, they fail to pull their weight. They do the donkey work. They are superbly loyal. They can be counted on to stand fast. But they hesitate when offered the perilous opportunity of responsibility, and certainly do not push for it.

This conventional load, which has been a very real obstacle—not the less real because hard to get to grips with—is, fortunately, much less heavy on the younger women. They have grown up in the atmosphere of emancipation. The " war-horses " of the fight for the suffrage sometimes complain, indeed, that the young take the vote, and so on, for granted. So they should. Its denial was an outrage. Its possession is elementary justice and common sense. The younger women have a hard enough task before them. They have got to win the next stage—real equality of opportunity and freedom of choice. How can they do it ?

They cannot do it at all so long as their view is bounded by their own sex. It was one of the major hardships of the suffrage fight that it compelled women to think and act in sex terms. That phase is over, and well over. It is good that the young ones breathe naturally in an air in which women and men are working comrades. So long as the problem which women workers present is thought of in terms of women only, no sound conclusion can be reached.

That is why the arguments about freedom of choice, as set out above in the preceding pages, remain, on the positive side, remote from actual circumstances, although drearily near on them in the negative. It is true that marriage does not solve the employment problem for the married, in a very large proportion of cases, and cannot solve it for the " superfluous " single, any more than for widowed or deserted wives. It is equally true that work, under actual conditions, is for women as for men, not a matter of choice but of necessity. It is true that women do not get an equal chance in industry, and true that girls do not get an equal chance in education. Yet this picture of in-equalities and hardships, although true enough in fact, is, somehow, not quite authentic. Something has been left out, which robs it of reality.

The falsification—for it amounts to that, although nothing of the sort is intended—arises from an effort to look at the woman's problem as though it were separate from the man's. It is, for instance, quite accurate to state that political freedom has not brought women economic freedom. Certainly it has not. But is the woman's case, in this, different from the man's? Has political brought economic freedom to men? Only to a limited extent. To the extent to which, through association and organisation, they have won it for themselves. The individual workman, if he tries to stand by and for himself, has little more freedom or scope than the individual workwoman. Workmen banded together in self-governing, democratic groups have a large measure of freedom, and a large measure of control over their own destiny ; they have in their hands the instrument through which they can win more. But the measure of their strength and their freedom is their power to stand together. That gives pride, self-respect, dignity, capability to master the great problems with which they are confronted.

Here, quite literally, the man's cause is the woman's, as the woman's cause is the man's. So long as they stay outside the associations of their fellow-workers and of the men whose companions they are within them, women are compelled to fulfil the dread dual function of being, for themselves and their companions, at once the executioner and the executed. They pull down the men's standards, and, by the same act, their own. The low wages of women at work are not only a burden upon women ; they are a drag upon men. Because the wages of men are lower than they need to be to support a growing family, women are forced into the labour market themselves, or confronted with an impossible task within the home.

Those who fight for fair treatment and freedom of choice for women, without at the same time, and as part of the same impulse, fighting for fair treatment and freedom of choice for men, are beating their heads against a wall. It is a potent and ancient wall ; the wall of that strange system of distribution of the fruits of common labour which, by giving to the many too little and to the few too much, actually restricts the available total to be shared. Fantastic as it may appear, yet it is true that inadequate consuming power in the hands of the great majority of the citizens is the main force that holds back the vast potential capacities for production of goods and services offered by the alliance of scientific discovery and human energy. Except on toil dedicated to the feverish supply of the instruments of mutual destruction, modern communities cannot keep their peoples busy. Yet the wheels of production could be set and kept revolving were they once fully set to the simple and primary task of giving to every home the elements of reasonable comfort.

On this fundamental and essential change, the future of women as workers and their freedom of choice in work plainly depends. When the basic wage of man or woman covers necessaries, then and only then will work within the home recover its dignity and its satisfaction, its claim on the community for recognition as work, which is its due. In practice and in idea, woman's cause is man's and man's, woman's.

The champion of that common cause is, of course, the Trade Union. The Trade Union is as important to the woman in the home as to the woman in industry. In its steady struggle for better conditions and for the just price for the job, it is fighting her battle, as well as that of the paid worker. In its struggle for political change that will cause both a fairer distribution of the national product, and a greater product, it is also fighting her battle.

The battle is, and is bound to be, primarily economic. But those who join the battle for economic freedom fight for and win personal freedom—freedom of mind and spirit—in the process.

In the Trade Union, moreover, the needs of women at work and of the woman in the home find themselves reconciled. There are black spots that need to be wiped out of the Union picture. The attitude of spinner, engineers, and compositors, to cite the outstanding instances of sex exclusion, is out of date, out of line with general Trade Union policy, and, in the long run, injurious to the members of these Unions. Once the principle of the rate for the job—and the maintenance of standards of skilled labour—is accepted, no Trade Union has anything to fear from admitting women. On the contrary, it has much to gain as well as to give.

The Unions which try to keep women out are to-day in a tiny minority. They can fairly be disregarded, since their conversion to the more general view is only a matter of time. If they are left out, it is incontestable that hope and decent conditions both for women at work and for the woman in the home depend on Trade Union action. To make that action fully effective, women must come inside. Outside, they weaken the one force that can free them and their menfolk.

Here, there are three outstanding points to be made. Through Trade Union action, and only through Trade Union action, adequate wages, tolerable hours, and decent working conditions can be won both for the men, on whom the life of the woman in the home depends, and for the women who work.

First, low wages for men are the main cause of hardship in the home. It is not at the period when it most needs the mother, because there are young children, that she, as things now are, should be compelled to go out and leave them, in order to eke out the father's insufficient earnings. Not choice on her part or on his, but hard necessity, brings the socially harmful family wage into existence.

The problem of the adjustment of resources to the needs of a growing family is one of great difficulty ; it is a problem in many middle-class homes, as well as for all wage-earners. This is not the place for a discussion of the pros and cons of a system of Family Allowances, although it may be noted that in Soldiers' Allowances, as in the Social Services, there is a movement in that direction. It is certain that only on a nation-wide basis, and under most strict Trade Union supervision, can such a plan be worked fairly and to the benefit of those concerned: indeed, it is questionable whether it can be grafted on to private ownership and management.

Second, and even more obvious is the interest of the woman who works. She has indeed everything to gain from Trade Union membership, both practically and emotionally, in her work and as a human being. For her, in fact, it is a first necessity.

Finally, every citizen, man and woman, has an interest in Trade Unionism. These great associations, democratic in structure and practice, and built up through strenuous and unselfish corporate effort, in which hundreds of unknown men and women have given all they have and are an indispensable and permanent part of the free community. It is sometimes suggested that Trade Unions are a transitional form : that once, through the combination of political and industrial action, the first main steps towards Socialism have been taken, the Trade Unions, as such, will wither and disappear.

Nothing could be further from the truth. Under Socialism, the free and varied associations of citizens will be more and not less important. Loyalty to the State must not become exclusive : that way Totalitarian madness lies. The association of workers for comradeship and counsel, as well as for social justice remains valuable under socialisation, because associations represent a focus of free discussion, a force making for mental growth and human fellowship, for tolerance and moral development. Socialism must not be static. It must not be tyrannical. It must not bring us a mechanical order that leaves no room for experiment or growth. The Trade Union will help to keep it clear of all these perils : and to secure that freedom grows. For it is the glory and special mark of democracy, of which Trade Unionism is a vital expression, that it, and it alone, is a kind of government that grows and promotes growth. Its form can never be finally fixed. It looks always to the future, and provides the instrument by which that future can be realised.

CHAPTER XI

AND NOW ?

N<small>OT</small> yet is it possible to make any useful survey, however broad and tentative, of the work of women under war conditions. Least of all under the peculiar conditions of this war. It was not until 1917 that there was any large-scale call on women in the last war, and any attempt, in 1917, to depict their activities would have been out of date as soon as it was written. It is so, in even greater measure, in 1941. We are now on the threshold only of the big transference of women to men's work which is bound to have far-reaching consequences. Idle to guess at what their effect may be.

All that can be done here is to note certain vital points of difference. This can be said, with assurance : in 1941 the status and conditions of women in the whole war effort of the nation are better than they were at any time in the 1914–18 war.

For the measure of fair treatment they now enjoy women workers have mainly to thank the Trade Union leaders, men and women, who upheld their cause, first in the years between 1918 and 1939, and then since the outbreak of war. Above all, they have to thank a band of women organisers who have, quite unsparing of themselves, devoted time, energy and infinite hard work and patience to the task of strengthening the Trade Union organisation of women, and of influencing their male colleagues inside the Unions to realise the importance of bringing women inside and treating them

176

as equals when they are inside. To mention names would be invidious : those of Anne Loughlin, Florence Hancock, Dorothy Elliot stand out as nationally known ; there are many more, working in particular trades, in particular localities, to whose unselfish and untiring devotion the result is due. They have never let go, however hard the task ; the debt all women owe to them is enormous.

Certainly the increased strength of Trade Unions themselves in the years between 1918 and 1939, and the steady conversion of Trade Union leaders to the view that the interests of men and women workers are indissolubly interlocked, created a position from the start strikingly different from that of 1914–18.

1939, of course, saw many 1914 features reappear, among them unemployment. This unemployment was especially severe and protracted in the case of women. Evacuation, dispersal, and dismissals caused widespread and lasting. dislocation. The luxury trades contracted sharply, and have not recovered ; the amusement industries, and those dependent on or related to them, like hotels and restaurants, shared the same fate. The office worker and the shop assistant found themselves " redundant ". The orderly calling up of men, under the operation of the Conscription Act, while it prevented the more glaring confusion of 1914, and slowly absorbed the male unemployed, hardly affected the unemployment of women, although it did create, in many cases, a shortage of skilled labour of particular kinds.

There was, of course, a repetition of the old-time clamour, from persons eager to be patriotic at other people's expense, for the hurried drafting of women into all sorts of employments where they would be cheap.

This was staunchly resisted. The Trade Unions stood firm for two points : the largest practical absorption of the unemployed, male and female, with schemes of training, to recall lost skill ; and the establishment, for " substitute " labour, of conditions that would safeguard what had been won through long years of organised effort.

In the first eight months of war, partly as the result of a wrong general policy, time was wasted, effort was wasted and Trade Union experience was wasted, through a failure to bring the Unions into partnership. Their help was available ; it was not used. When the National Government was formed, however, under Mr. Churchill, in May 1940, production was, at last, placed on a wartime footing, and Trade Unions were, at length, fully associated with the national effort. The Emergency Powers (Defence) Bill, introduced on May 22nd in that year, gave the Government powers over the entire resources of the country. At the same time, Mr. Attlee, in introducing the Bill as Deputy Leader of the House of Commons, assured the workers that their rights would remain alive, and would be secured by an addition to the fair wages clause whereby any employers who did not restore customs or conditions set aside for the duration would be ineligible to go on the list of Government contractors.

Substitution was, of course, the major issue. Here, Trade Unionism has secured very important agreements in three major lines of employment. In the Boot and Shoe Trade, in Engineering industries, and in transport, the principle of the rate for the job has been established. Women doing work normally done by men get the same rate, the same bonus, and the same cost-of-living addition as the men get.

And Now?

In the Boot and Shoe Trade, this is part of the Agreement accepted by the National Joint Conference of employers and employed in the trade, in January 1940. Paragraph 10 of this Agreement lays it down that where females are employed (in the clicking, press, lasting and finishing departments, in which male labour is, in peace-time, almost exclusively employed), " they shall receive the wage-rates appropriate to men doing similar work ".

In the Engineering trades, negotiations had been going on for many months before the outbreak of war. As a result of long and complicated discussions, a wage position for women was achieved that is infinitely better than they reached even in the latter stages of the 1914 war. The negotiations were conducted between the Engineering Employers Federation, on the one side, and, on the other, the National Union of General and Municipal Workers and the Transport Workers Federation, these being the two Unions with the greater number of women in the engineering trades among their membership. In May 1940, terms were finally agreed, which were also signed by the Amalgamated Engineering Union, although, since it does not admit women to membership, it was not a party to the negotiations. The gist of this agreement is that, after a probationary and training period has been completed, qualified women get the same rate as that paid to the men whom they replace. The women who come in are regarded as temporarily employed ; it is part of the stand of the A E U that women are not to be taken in while suitable men are available, and that, after the war, the men would be re-instated. Women who have completed their probationary period, in three defined stages, and can work without special supervision, then receive the basic rate and the bonus appropriate to the men whom they replace. At the same time, special rates were negotiated for women doing what is rated normally as women's work.

In Transport, the Unions stood out, from the first, for the rate for the job for substituted women. For many weeks, the employers resisted this claim ; finally, the issue was referred to the Industrial Court for arbitration. The upshot was a great triumph : the award of the Court lays down the vitally important principle that the rates and conditions already fixed by agreement for adult male conductors should apply to women. The women must be over 18. For the first six months of service, women of 21 receive not less than 90 per cent. of the adult male's commencing rate ; thereafter, the scale of pay and increment applicable to adult male conductors ; those taken on at 18, stay on the 90 per cent. until they are 21. The guaranteed week may be 40 hours instead of 48 ; time worked in excess of 40 hours is to be paid at the men's overtime rates. Here is a very important precedent.

The principle as regards wages which has been laid down and operated in these three major industries, is likely to have a lasting as well as temporary effect, so far as organised workers are concerned. Of course, there are loopholes ; on this process and on that, the question will be raised, Is the job the woman is doing really the same as the man did ? Vigilance on the part of the Union will be required. Its effectiveness must depend in very large measure on the degree of unionisation in the industries affected. But the difference between now and 1914–18 is striking.

On hours, again, the position is very much better than in 1914. Both for organised and unorganised

workers in war industries, extension of hours beyond the
legal limit can only take place by consultation and by
the agreement of the Unions, who have established—
and this is very important—a general control over hours
worked, and the right to speak on behalf of those
outside their own membership. True, there was a
period, in the summer of 1940 and after the collapse of
France, when this control was waived, and very long
hours were worked. This spurt and the waiving of
conditions was, however, a spontaneous gesture on the
part of the workers themselves, who responded with
glorious enthusiasm and self-sacrifice to their country's
need. Since then, the extension of the provision of the
Factories Act to all establishments transferred to the
control of the Ministry of Labour has limited hours ;
only by Trade Union agreement, under the Engineering
Emergency Order, can they be extended. Such is the
theory ; and such, in a considerable number, perhaps a
majority of cases, is the practice. Idle, however, to
pretend there are not disorganised patches, where the
provisions laid down for the protection of the workers
are evaded.

The same applies to conditions of work. By and
large, one can say that the position here is, again,
infinitely better than in the last war. The Factory and
Welfare Department of the Ministry of Labour has set
standards that are, gradually, coming into effect ;
lighting and ventilation (especially important under
black-out conditions, and the continuance of work
during periods of alert) are being watched ; canteens
are being introduced ; there is a general, instructed
concern for the health of workers, especially of women
workers, which was notably absent before. The
influence of Mr. Bevin as Minister of Labour makes

itself vigorously felt. At the same time, the realisation of the desires and intentions of the Minister depends, to a very large extent, on continuous watchfulness and activity by the Unions—as on the degree to which the workers themselves are Union members.

Certainly, the position of the industrial woman worker is, in many respects, better looked after than is that of the woman in the Services or the householder. The provisions of the scheme for Compensation for Civilian Injuries (Air Raids) differentiate harshly against the woman who, whether or no she is gainfully employed, receives 7s. a week less than the man, purely on grounds of her sex. Women workers under Civil Defence schemes, like the women in the Auxiliary Services, only receive 75 per cent. of the men's rates. These are gross anomalies. They register the old view that a woman's keep, even where she is a homekeeper with young children, is less than a man's.

Nevertheless, there is a far stronger public opinion in favour of equal treatment than ever in the late war. The time is again giving proof of the painful paradox that war conditions are women's opportunity. This is especially true of this war. For two main reasons. The first is practical. The fact that civilians are in the front line both of suffering and action means that women are playing as much needed a part as men. They are indispensable in the Civil Defence services from A R P downwards. Their organisation, through the practical genius of Lady Reading, in the W V S (Women's Voluntary Service), has provided an invaluable body of helpers and servers, quite distinct from the " kind ladies " of the past. They are going to be needed, more and more, to carry on the nation's work ; and the nation knows it.

The second reason is moral. This is a war for democracy, for human freedom, for the happiness that can be achieved through co-operation and must be lost if egotistical tyranny tramples on the many in the interests of a handful of witch doctors, who deny to the mind the right to think its own thoughts. Women, whether they work in the home or at the bench, cannot help symbolising the great issue at stake—Civilisation against force : life against death for the human spirit. They are, of course, inferior where the weight of brawn and muscle, the drive of brutality, is the one qualification for the useful slave. In a regime of force, they go to the wall : and every human value goes with them. For them, obviously, democracy is the line of life. Under it they are free to grow in equality of contribution to the common cause : under it they make no claim to any special rights ; only to that opportunity of service and fellowship which makes them partners with men.

APPENDIX

CENSUS OF 1931

A. POPULATION
Female

	1921	1931
Total population . . .	19,811,460	20,819,367
„ „ over 14 . .	14,959,282	16,410,894
Occupied over 14 . . .	5,036,727	5,606,043
„ between 12 and 13 .	28,605	—

B. WOMEN IN THE OCCUPATIONAL GROUPS

	1921	1931
Agriculture	83,052	55,683 (including 17,367 farmers and 16 foremen)
Mining	3,364	2,561
Non-Metallurgical Manufacturers	774	1,205
Bricks, Pottery, Glass . . .	20,931	25,418
Chemicals	3,604	4,224
Metals (not Electro) . . .	84,848	96,120
Electro	14,494	11,511
Electricians	13,396	28,445
Watches, Clocks, Scientific Instruments	1,995	1,568
Skins and Leather . . .	19,662	24,049
Textiles	557,431	574,094
Dress Goods	533,287	542,809
Food, Drink, Tobacco . .	63,988	74,888
Wood and Furniture . . .	17,308	19,734
Paper and Cardboard. . .	51,431	63,994
Printers and Photogravures . .	33,888	37,958
Builders, etc.	775	445 (including pottery)
Painters and Decorators . .	25,676	36,091
Other Materials. . . .	18,445	19,071

	1921	1931
Undefined Materials	17,474	14,801
Transport	63,580	68,899
Commercial (not clerks) . .	504,264	604,833
(including 600,000 proprietary managers of retail businesses)		
Public Administration (not typists)	71,881	2,906
Professional (not clerical) . .	348,461	389,359
(including 118,909 nurses 181,806 teachers)		
Entertainment and Sport . .	19,773	22,369
Personal Service . . .	1,676,425	1,926,978
(including 127,647 laundry, 146,000 charwomen 1,332,224 domestic servants)		
Clerks, Typists	429,921	579,945
Warehouse	128,710	155,794
Engines (stationary) . . .	2	409
Others	243,863	219,482
Retired or not gainfully employed	10,634,473	10,804,851

APPENDIX TO CHAPTER III

WOMEN IN THE PRINCIPAL UNIONS
(as returned to the 71st Trade Union Congress,
September, 1939)

The figures below cover pre-war conditions and are given in preference to those for 1940, for that reason.

Group	Women	Men
1. MINING AND QUARRYING.		
2. RAILWAYS :		
National Union of Railwaymen .	2,006	364,653
Railway Clerks Association . .	6,350	57,756
3. TRANSPORT :		
National Union of Seamen . .	927	48,562
Transport and General Workers .	33,481	601,519
5. ENGINEERING :		
Engineering and Shipbuilding Draughtsmen	1,139	18,171
6. IRON AND STEEL AND MINOR METALS :		
Bedstead Workers . . .	54	398
Cutlery Union	80	420
File Trades, Sheffield A.U. . .	481	986
Gold and Silver	474	3,297
Goldsmiths	81	1,040
Iron and Steel Confederation .	1,321	84,131
Lock and Metal Workers . .	1,328	2,012
Spring Trapmakers . . .	20	70
Wire Drawers	76	6,329
Wool Sheer Workers . . .	4	98
7. BUILDING, WOODWORKING, FURNISHING :		
Bedding Trade Workers . .	60	440
Furnishing Trades Association .	930	20,348
Packing Case Makers . . .	323	3,222
Sign, Glass, and Ticket Writers .	4	946
Upholsterers	2,794	66,229

Group	Women	Men
8. PRINTING AND PAPER		
Monotype Casters . . .	4	820
National Society of Operative Printers	6,481	21,173
National Union of Printers, Book-		
binders and Paper Workers .	31,000	40,000
Press Telegraphists . . .	10	544
Typographical Association (Scotland)	1,700	5,300
Wall Paper Workers' Union . .	830	2,150
9. COTTON :		
Bleachers, Twisters and Drawers .	198	4,084
Card, Blowing and Ring Room .	36,776	9,193
Textile Warehousemen . .	1,300	6,000
Weavers Association . . .	70,736	17,683
10. OTHER TEXTILES :		
Dyers and Bleachers . . .	35,972	43,040
Engravers	198	1,676
Jute and Flax Workers . .	6,000	2,000
Lace Operatives	1,125	1,215
Power Loom Carpet Weavers .	2,700	1,600
Warpdressers (Leeds) . . .	30	210
Weavers and Wool Textile Workers		
(Saddleforth)	845	706
11. CLOTHING :		
Felt Hat Trimmers . . .	3,429	—
Hosiery (4 local Unions) . .	11,797	3,800
Waterproof Garments . . .	870	269
Tailors and Garment Workers .	66,807	23,508
12. LEATHER :		
Boot and Shoe Makers . .	20	1,230
Boot and Shoe Operatives (N.U.)	30,968	56,019
„ „ „ (Perivale)	3,127	6,256
Glovers	308	1,246
Leather Workers	990	6,483
13. GLASS, POTTERY, CHEMICALS ; FOOD, DRINK, TOBACCO ; DISTRIBUTION :		
Bakers	1,200	16,800
„ (Scottish)	314	8,379
Blind (National League) . .	1,630	4,084
Brushmakers	600	2,000
Butchers	90	5,876
Cigar and Tobacco Workers . .	1,650	550
Commercial Travellers . . .	3	593

Group	Women	Men
Co-operative Officials . . .	71	5,901
Distributive and Allied Workers .	54,119	128,514
Pottery Workers	14,292	8,583
Retail Booksellers. . . .	794	2,212
Shop Assistants	25,514	51,087

14. AGRICULTURE :

	Women	Men
Agricultural Workers . . .	500	44,500

15. PUBLIC EMPLOYEES :

	Women	Men
National Union of County Officers	6,250	6,746
Mental Hospital and Institutional Workers	7,398	11,974
National Union of Public Employees	4,777	45,372
Women Public Health Officers .	2,183	—

16. NON-MANUAL WORKERS :

	Women	Men
Cine-Technicians	110	1,102
Clerks, National Union of . .	5,509	8,708
Film Artists. . . .	294	496
Insurance Officials . . .	7,614	13,676
Theatrical and Kine-Employees .	4,714	8,694
Women Clerks and Secretaries .	2,500	—

17. GENERAL WORKERS :

	Women	Men
General and Municipal Workers .	43,321	373,810
Laundry Workers . . .	349	41
Salt Workers	250	1,547